THE AUTOBIOGRAPHY
OF AN ELECTRON

THE AUTOBIOGRAPHY OF AN ELECTRON

CHARLES ROBERT GIBSON

ISBN: 978-93-89614-05-3

Published: 1911

LECTOR HOUSE LLP
E-MAIL: lectorpublishing@gmail.com

A Well-known Phenomenon Produced by Electrons

A sudden discharge of electrons from cloud to cloud, or from cloud to the earth, constitutes what we call "lightning."

THE AUTOBIOGRAPHY OF AN ELECTRON.

WHEREIN THE SCIENTIFIC IDEAS OF THE PRESENT TIME ARE EXPLAINED IN AN INTERESTING AND NOVEL FASHION

BY

CHARLES R. GIBSON, F.R.S.E.

Author Of "Scientific Ideas Of To-Day," "Electricity Of To-Day" "The Romance Of Modern Electricity," &C. &C.

ILLUSTRATED

1911

PREFACE

Although text-books of science may appear to the general reader to be "very dry" material, there is no doubt that, when scientific facts and theories are put into everyday language, the general reader is genuinely interested. The reception accorded to the present author's *Scientific Ideas of To-day* bears out this fact. While that volume explains, in non-technical language, the latest scientific theories, it aims at giving a fairly full account, which, of course, necessitates going into a great deal of detail. That the book has been appreciated by very varied classes of readers is evident from the large numbers of appreciative letters received from different quarters. But the author believes that if the story of modern science were told in a still more popular style, it would serve a further useful purpose. For there are readers who do not care to go into details, and yet would like to take an intelligent interest in the scientific progress of the present day. Some of those readers do not wish to trouble about names and dates, while the mere mention of rates of vibration and such-like is a worry to them. They wish a book which they may read with the same ease as an interesting novel. Hence the form of the present volume.

The author is indebted to Professor James Muir, M.A., D.Sc., of the Glasgow and West of Scotland Technical College, and to H. Stanley Allen, M.A., D.Sc., Senior Lecturer in Physics at King's College, University of London, for very kindly reading the proof-sheets. The author is indebted further to Professor Muir in connection with some of the illustrations, and for others to Dixon and Corbitt and R. S. Newall, Ltd., Glasgow; Siemens Schuckert Werke, Berlin.

CONTENTS

CHAPTER I

WHAT THE STORY IS ABOUT

CHAPTER II

THE ELECTRON'S PREFACE

CHAPTER III

THE NEW ARRIVAL

CHAPTER IV

SOME GOOD SPORT

CHAPTER V

MY EARLIEST RECOLLECTIONS

CHAPTER VI

MAN PAYS US SOME ATTENTION

CHAPTER VII

A STEADY MARCH

CHAPTER VIII

A USEFUL DANCE

CHAPTER IX

HOW WE CARRY MAN'S NEWS

CHAPTER XV

WE SEND MESSAGES FROM THE STARS

CHAPTER XVI

HOW MAN PROVED OUR EXISTENCE

CHAPTER XVII

MY X-RAY EXPERIENCES

CHAPTER XVIII

OUR RELATIONSHIP TO THE ATOMS

CHAPTER XIX

HOW WE MADE THE WORLD TALK

CHAPTER XX

CONCLUSION

LIST OF ILLUSTRATIONS

CHAPTER I

WHAT THE STORY IS ABOUT

The Scribe introduces the Electron to the reader. He has something to
say also about the mysterious æther which pervades all space. He
emphasises the fact that the electron is a real existing thing

The reason for writing this story is given in the Preface, but the title is so
strange that the reader will wish naturally to know what the story is about. What
is an electron? Is it an imaginary thing, or is it a reality?

One of the reasons for writing this story in its present form is to help the reader to realise that electrons are not mythical, but real existing things, and by far the
most interesting things we know anything about. The discovery of electrons has
shed a new light upon the meaning of very many things which have been puzzles
until now. They give us a reasonable explanation of the cause of light and colour.
They provide a new idea of the constitution of matter. They enable us to picture an
electric current, and they give us definite, though by no means final, answers to the
why and wherefore of magnetism, chemical union, and radio-activity.

The story is imaginary only in so far that one of the electrons itself is supposed
to tell the tale. But in the endeavour to make the story interesting, there has been
no sacrifice of accuracy in the statements of fact.

While all names and dates, and many other details, have been kept out rigidly
from the story, a note of the more important of these has been added in an Appendix for the sake of those readers who may wish to refer to them.

It will be well to introduce the electron to the reader before leaving it to speak
for itself. We have definite experimental proof of the existence of electrons, and yet
it is very difficult to realise their existence, for two reasons. In the first place, they
are so infinitesimally small. We count a microbe a small thing; we can see it only
with the aid of a very powerful microscope. Yet that little speck of matter contains
myriads of particles or *atoms*. An atom of matter is therefore an inconceivably little
thing, but even that is a great giant compared to an electron. Our second difficulty
in realising the existence of an electron is that it is not any form of what we call
matter; it is a particle of *electricity*, whatever that may be.

From the earliest experiments it became evident that there were two distinct
kinds of electricity. These were described by the pioneer workers as *positive* and
negative electricities. To-day we have definite experimental proof that negative
electricity is composed of separate particles or units. Just as matter is composed

of invisible atoms, so also is negative electricity of an atomic nature. These particles of negative electricity have been christened electrons, *electron* being the Greek word for *amber*, from which man first obtained electricity. Of course no one can ever hope to see an electron, but physicists have been able to determine its size and *mass*, its electric charge, and the speeds at which it moves.

While it has been known for more than a century that *light* is merely waves in the all-pervading æther of space, set up by incandescent bodies, it has been a puzzle always how matter could cause waves in the æther, as it offers no resistance to the movement of matter through it. Here we are on the back of a great planet, flying through space at the enormous rate of one thousand miles per minute, and yet our flimsy atmospheric blanket is in no way disturbed by the æther through which we are flying. In the following story we shall see that these electrons help us towards a solution of this and many other problems; they provide the missing link between matter and the æther.

But what is this *æther* of which one hears so much in these days? The truth is we know nothing of its nature. We cannot say whether it is lighter than the lightest gas or denser than the densest solid. The æther, whatever it may be, is as real as the air we breathe. It is the medium which brings us light and heat from the sun, and which carries our wireless telegraph and telephone messages. The whole universe is moving in this great æther ocean.

In order to make the electron's story perfectly intelligible to every reader, I have added a short explanatory note at the beginning of each chapter. These notes merely state the facts about which the electron is speaking.

To make the electron's story as realistic as possible, it has been necessary to give the imaginary electron perfect freedom of knowledge concerning itself and its surroundings. In our schooldays we had to write the autobiographies of steel pens, and such-like, but these inanimate things had to be endowed with powers of thought, feeling, and desire. It is very important, however, to remember that an electron is a particle of negative electricity—*a real existing thing*.

CHAPTER II

THE ELECTRON'S PREFACE

The Electron explains the reason why it has written its autobiography

While many scientific men now understand our place in the universe, we electrons are anxious that every person should know the very important part which we play in the workaday world. It was for this reason that my fellow-electrons urged me to write my own biography. My difficulty has been to find a scribe who would put down my story in the way I desired. The first man with whom I opened negotiations wished me to give him dates and names of which I knew nothing. And he asked such stupid questions about where I was born and who my parents were, as if I were flesh and blood.

I am pleased to say that my relationship with the scribe who has put down my story in the following pages has been of the most friendly description. Apart from a little tiff which we had at the outset, there has been no difference of opinion. He complained that I related things in too abstract a form. However, we got over the difficulty by a compromise; I have allowed him to place what he calls "The Scribe's Note" at the beginning of each chapter, but it will be understood clearly that these are merely convenient embellishments, and that I am responsible for the story of my own experiences.

CHAPTER III
THE NEW ARRIVAL

The Electron points out who the new arrival is really. It relates an amusing experience. It tells how man disturbed electrons before he discovered their existence. An ancient experiment, and what the wise men of the East thought about it. How electrons are responsible for the electrification of any object. Handled by a new experimenter, they surprise man. Man becomes of special interest to the electrons

THE SCRIBE'S NOTE ON CHAPTER THREE

It will be well to keep clearly in mind that an electron is a real particle of negative electricity.

Electrons have been discovered only within recent years.

No matter from what substances we take them, they are always identical in every respect.

Some electrons are attached to the atoms of matter in such a way that they may be removed easily from one object to another.

When a surplus of these detachable electrons is crowded on to any object, we say that it is charged with negative electricity.

We speak of the other object, which has lost these same electrons, as being charged with positive electricity.

In this chapter the electron refers to the old-world experiment in which a piece of amber when rubbed attracts any light object to it.

For many ages man believed this to be a special property belonging to amber alone.

One of Queen Elizabeth's physicians discovered that this property was common to all substances.

It is most amusing to me and my fellow-electrons to hear intelligent people speak of us as though we were new arrivals on this planet. Dear me! We were here for countless ages before man put in an appearance. I wonder if any man can realise that we have been on the move ever since the foundations of this world were laid. It is man himself who is the new arrival.

It does seem strange to us that men should be so distinctly different from one another. We electrons are at a decided disadvantage, for we are all identical in every respect. I have no individual name—it would serve no purpose. Even if you could see me, you could not distinguish me from any other electron. I wonder sometimes if men appreciate the great advantage they have in possessing individual names. I was impressed with this thought one fine summer morning. While I was riding on the back of a particle of gas in the atmosphere, I was carried through the open window of a nursery just as the under-nurse was putting the room in order. A little later there was some commotion in the nursery, for the young mother and her mother had come to see the twin daughters being bathed by the nurses. The grandmother happened to remark how very much alike the two little infants were. She said laughingly to the head nurse that she must be careful not to get the children mixed. But the big brother, aged five years, remarked that it would not matter really how much they were mixed until they got their names. Sometimes I wish we electrons did differ from one another, so that we might each possess an individual name, but no doubt it is necessary for us all to be exactly alike.

Long before man had discovered us, he caused us deliberately to do certain things. He was mystified by the results of his experiments, for he was not aware of our presence. A few of my fellow-electrons have rather hazy recollections of being disturbed while clinging to a piece of amber. They had been disturbed often before in a similar way, by being rubbed against a piece of woollen cloth, and the result had been always that a number of electrons let go their hold upon the cloth and crowded on to the amber. The overcrowding was uncomfortable, but it happened usually that the surplus electrons found some means of escape to the earth, where there is no need of excessive crowding.

On the occasion to which I refer, it so happened that the rubbing had been unusually vigorous and prolonged, so that the electrons were crowded on to the amber in great numbers. In their endeavour to escape they produced a strain or stress in the surrounding æther, and this caused a small piece of straw, which was lying within the disturbed area, to be forced towards the amber.

What attracted the attention of the electrons was that the man who was holding the piece of amber removed the clinging straw and replaced it exactly where it had been lying. In the meantime he had been handling the amber, and many of the crowded electrons had managed to make a bolt for the earth by way of the man's body. They did this so very quietly that the man did not feel any sensation. However, as soon as the amber was rubbed again, a similar crowd provided the same attractive property. We electrons became impatient to hear what man would say of our work, for it was apparent that he had noticed the movements of the straw. You will hardly believe me when I tell you to what decision these wise men of the East came. They declared that, in rubbing the amber, it had received heat and life. As if life could be originated in any such simple manner!

You can picture our disappointment when we found that man was going to ignore our presence. Occasionally we were given opportunities of displaying our abilities in drawing light objects towards pieces of rubbed amber. But the funny thing was that man got hold of the stupid idea that this attractive property belonged to the amber instead of to us. If he had only tried pieces of sulphur, resin, or glass, he would have found that these substances would have acted just as well. You see it was not really the substance, but we electrons who were the active agents.

We had given up all hope of being discovered, when news came along that a learned man was on the hunt for us. He was crowding us on to all sorts of substances. He rubbed a piece of glass with some silk, and at first he was surprised greatly to see light objects jump towards the excited glass. Of course, we were not surprised in the very least. The only thing that amused us was to find that he was making out a list of the different substances which showed attractive properties when rubbed. He could not, evidently, get away from the idea that it was the substances themselves that became attractive.

We were sorry that the poor experimenter wasted so much time and energy in trying to crowd us on to a piece of metal rod. He rubbed and he rubbed that metal, but it would attract nothing, and I shall tell you the reason. You know that we electrons hate overcrowding; indeed we always separate from one another as far as possible when there is no force pulling us together. We only crowded on to the amber because we could not help ourselves; we had no way of escape, for amber is a substance we cannot pass through. But we have no difficulty whatever in making our way along a piece of metal, and as soon as the rubbing began, some electrons moved off the metal by way of the man's arm and body to make room for those being crowded on to the metal from the rubber. And so there never was any overcrowding, and consequently no straining of the æther. But it was not long before we found that man had succeeded in cutting off our way of escape. He had attached a glass handle to the metal rod, and we were compelled to overcrowd upon the metal as we could not pass through the glass handle. Neighbouring light objects were attracted by the excited or "electrified" metal. Even this demonstration did not put man upon our track.

Perhaps I should explain in passing, that when a glass rod is rubbed with a silk handkerchief we crowd on to the silk, and not on to the glass. This leaves the glass rod short of electrons, and the æther is strained so that light objects are attracted. Man did notice that there was some difference between a piece of amber and a piece of glass when these were excited. What the difference was he could not imagine, but to distinguish the two different conditions he said that the amber was charged with *negative* electricity and the glass with *positive* electricity.

From that time forward man became of special interest to us. We felt sure that sooner or later he was bound to recognise that we were at work behind the scenes. It seemed to us, however, that man was desperately slow in turning his attention towards us, and we tried to waken him up in a rather alarming fashion, as I shall relate in the succeeding chapter.

CHAPTER IV

SOME GOOD SPORT

The Electron explains how man succeeded in crowding them together, with some rather exciting results from the overcrowding. One historical incident. Man's fear of the consequences. How a party of electrons wrecked a church steeple. An unfortunate accident

THE SCRIBE'S NOTE ON CHAPTER FOUR

Men began to make glass plate machines for producing electrification on a larger scale.

The electric spark is produced.

The electron tells the story of the first attempt to store electricity in a glass jar.

This is what we do now by means of a Leyden jar.

A sudden expulsion of electrons from one object to another is called a discharge of electricity.

Lightning is a discharge of electrons from a cloud to the earth or from cloud to cloud.

In repeating Franklin's experiment of drawing electricity from thunder-clouds, a Russian professor received a fatal shock.

Now I must tell you of a surprise in which I took an active part. Some man thought he would separate a great crowd of us from our friends. Of course, he did not think really of *us*, but whatever he may have supposed he was doing, he succeeded in accumulating greater crowds of us together than he had done previously. He managed this by making simple machines to do the rubbing for him on a larger scale. The result was really too much for us; we were kept crowding on to a sort of brass comb arrangement from which we could not escape, as the metal was attached to a glass support. Talk about overcrowding! I had never experienced the like before, and I felt sure some catastrophe would happen. Suddenly there was a stampede, during which a great crowd of electrons forced their way across to a neighbouring object and thence to the earth. I can assure you it was no joke getting through the air. We all tried to leap together, but some of the crowd were forced back upon us; then bang forward we went again, back once more, and so on till we settled down to our normal condition. Of course all this surging to and fro occupied far less time than it takes to tell. Indeed, I could not tell you what a very small fraction of a second it took.

I wish you had seen the experimenter's surprise as we made this jump. We caused such a bombardment in the air that there was a bright spark accompanied by a regular explosion. Some men ran away with the idea that electricity was a mysterious fire, which only showed itself when it mixed with the atmosphere. Nothing delighted us more, after our own surprise was over, than to have a chance of repeating these explosions, to the alarm of the experimenters. But the best sport of all was to come, and when I heard of it I was so disappointed that I had not been one of the sporting party. It came about in the following way.

By permission of Dixon and Corbitt and R. S. Newall, Ltd.   *Glasgow*
Damage Done by a Party of Electrons
When a myriad of electrons is discharged suddenly from a

cloud to the earth, it happens sometimes that considerable damage is done. The above photograph is of a church steeple damaged by lightning in 1875. No lightning-conductor was provided, so the electrons had to get to earth by way of the steeple itself, with the disastrous result as shown.

One learned man thought he had hit upon a good idea. He tried to crowd a tremendous number of us into some water contained in a glass jar. Without condescending to think of us, he crowded an enormous number of electrons from one of his rubbing machines along a piece of chain which led them into water. The over-crowding was appalling, for it was impossible to escape through the glass vessel. Things had reached a terrible state, when the experimenter stopped the machine and put forward his hand to lift the chain out of the water. Now was the chance of escape, so the whole excited crowd made one wild rush to earth by way of the experimenter's body. The rapid surging to and fro of the crowd racked the man's muscles. I wish I had been there to see him jump; they say it was something grand. You can imagine how the little sinners enjoyed the joke; they knew they were safe, as man had no idea of their existence at that time.

Another man was foolhardy enough to try a similar experiment, and they say that his alarm was even greater; indeed, he swore he would not take another shock even for the crown of France. We were all eager to get opportunities of alarming man, not that we wished him any harm, but we thought he might pay us a little more attention.

I remember one occasion upon which some of us were boasting of what we had done in the way of alarming men, whereupon one fellow-electron rather be-littled our doings. He maintained that he had jumped all the way from a cloud to the earth, along with a crowd of other electrons. In doing so they had scared the inhabitants of a whole village, for they alighted upon the steeple of a church, and in their wild rush they played such havoc among the atoms composing the steeple that they did considerable outward damage to the great structure.

I may as well confess that we are not free agents in performing these gigantic jumps; we are compelled to go with the crowd when things are in such a state of stress. We simply cannot hold on to the atoms of matter upon which we happen to be located. It is only under very considerable pressure that we can perform this class of jump, and I beg to assure you that we are perfectly helpless in those cases where we have been dashed upon some poor creature with a message of death.

Alas! on one occasion I was one of a party who killed a very learned man. It was most distasteful to us; we could not possibly prevent it. He had erected a long rod which extended up into the air, and terminated at the lower end in his laboratory. Some of us who were in the upper atmosphere were forced on to this iron rod, and from past experience we quite expected that we should be subjected to a sudden expulsion to earth. Indeed we were waiting for the experimenter to provide us with a means of escape, when suddenly he brought his head too near to the end of the rod, and in a moment we were dashed to earth through his body. We learned with deep regret that the poor man had been robbed of his life.

To turn to something of a happier nature, I shall proceed to tell you of some of my earliest recollections. Remember I shall be speaking of a time long before man existed—even before this great planet was a solid ball.

CHAPTER V

MY EARLIEST RECOLLECTIONS

The Electron's story begins at a very far distant period, before this world had taken shape. The Electron was present when the atoms of matter were being formed. The birth of the moon. Something still to be discovered. The moulding of the planet. Boiling oceans. The electrons took an active part in making sea-water salt. The Electron explains why it has been chosen to write the story of itself and its fellows

THE SCRIBE'S NOTE ON CHAPTER FIVE

This great globe upon which we live was once a glowing mass of flaming gas.

It is possible that the whole solar system was once one great mass.

In any case, we have no doubt that the moon is simply the result of a part of our glowing mass having become detached.

In the hottest stars we find only the lightest atoms of matter, such as hydrogen gas, the atoms of heavier substances being found in stars which have begun to cool down.

The electrons have been present from the very beginning, and it is they who go to make up the atoms of matter.

We picture an atom of matter as a miniature solar system of revolving electrons.

There is doubtless a corresponding amount of positive electricity, but so far we have no evidence of its nature.

Before giving an account of the everyday duties which we perform, it may interest you to hear something of our early history.

Not only have we been on the move ever since the beginning of this world, but some of us have clear recollections of this planet long before it was a solid body. The whole world was a great ball of flaming gas. I have heard some fellow-electrons say that we were attached to a greater mass of incandescent gas before the beginning of this world, but I have no personal recollections of it. But one thing I do remember is a great upheaval which caused a large mass of gas to become detached from our habitation. Without any warning a great myriad of our fellow-electrons were carried away on this smaller mass. At first this detached mass circled around our greater mass at very close quarters, but we soon found that our friends were being carried farther and farther away, until they are now circling around this solid planet at a comparatively great distance. Man calls this detached mass *the moon*, and when I have heard children say in fun that they wish they could visit the man in the moon, I have longed to go and see how it fares with those fellow-electrons who seem to be separated from us in such a permanent manner.

After this exciting event, which I have heard described as "the birth of the moon," our great ball of flaming gas began to cool gradually. But you will be interested in what happened before the moon's birth. I saw a crowd of electrons suddenly congregate together along with *something* else which man has not discovered. Never mind the other part, but picture a number of electrons forming a little world of their own. There they went whirling around in a giddy dance. I saw these little worlds or "atoms" being formed all around, and I feel truly thankful now that I was not caught in the mad whirl, for these fellow-electrons have been kept hard at it ever since, imprisoned within a single atom. I have met a very few electrons who have escaped from within an atom, but I shall tell you about them later on.

The first thing I noticed was that each of the atoms had practically the same number of electrons in it. At that time I thought only in an abstract way, but since then I have learned that these were *hydrogen* atoms; hydrogen being the lightest substance known to man. Exactly what happened next I cannot recollect, but my attention was attracted later to larger congregations of electrons forming other little worlds of their own. These atoms were, of course, heavier than the hydrogen atoms. I saw quite a variety of different systems, of which I thought then in an abstract fashion, but which I know now to be atoms of *oxygen, nitrogen, carbon, iron, copper*, and so on. While man has given the atoms these distinguishing names, you will understand that the incidents which I am relating took place long before there was any appearance of solidity about our planet; these substances were all in a gaseous state.

After this, I recollect that there was a great envelope of water-vapour condensed around the planet. Some condensed into liquid water upon the surface of the globe, while part was suspended in the form of clouds. Some of my fellow-electrons acted as *nuclei* or foundations for the formation of the cloud particles. The water which condensed upon the earth settled down in the hollows, which had been produced previously by the immense pressure of the water-vapour envelope. We can hardly believe it is the same world.

You cannot imagine how strange it was to see the great oceans boiling and steaming; of course, they were fresh water then. I need hardly tell you that they have become salt only because the rivers have brought down sodium into them, and when these sodium atoms unite with chlorine atoms they form particles of common salt. I know all about this because we electrons play a very important part in all such combinations.

One very memorable recollection is that of life originating in the oceans. I wish

I could let you into the secret of *the origin of life*, but, according to the Creator's plan, man must find out for himself. Your guesses are all wide of the mark.

By the way, perhaps I should explain why I have been selected to write this biography. The first reason is that I am a free or detachable electron, and the second point in my favour is that I have had exceptional opportunities of seeing about me. I have heard men say that lookers-on see most of the game, and as I have witnessed the gradual evolution of things, you will understand that I have views of my own. A casual observer might think that things had deteriorated, for long ago there were immense monsters upon this planet, and these would put all modern creatures in the shade as far as size and strength are concerned. But one of the most interesting things to me has been to watch the evolution of man, and more especially the gradual development of his brain. Indeed, sometimes I have wished that I had happened to be an electron in the brain of a man; but, on the other hand, my career would not have been of the varied kind which it has been.

CHAPTER VI

MAN PAYS US SOME ATTENTION

The electrons are encouraged by one of the experiments made by man. They hope it may lead to their discovery, so that their services may be recognised. The Electron's experience in a vacuum tube. A disappointment and a revival of hope. A great declaration by one individual man. The Electron misjudges man. Mention of a great discovery. The christening of the electrons

THE SCRIBE'S NOTE ON CHAPTER SIX

Men found that by exhausting the air from glass globes or tubes it was possible to pass electric discharges through them, and in so doing some very beautiful luminous effects were produced within the vacuum tubes.

It was when experimenting with one of these tubes that a scientist suggested that radiant particles were being shot across the tube.

These particles were really electrons, but it was thought at that time that they were atoms of matter.

Another scientist declared, from certain mathematical calculations, that there existed extremely small particles of something around the atoms of matter, and that it was the motion of these in the æther which produced *light*.

People were not willing to accept this theory.

Some time later another scientist was able to prove by experiment that these particles did exist.

This was done by means of the spectroscope, as will be related by the electron in a later chapter.

From the little I have told you already of our experiences, you will see that men had been making many experiments in which we electrons took a very active part. It was disappointing that even although we had surprised man in so many different ways, he had never become suspicious of our presence. One day, however, we did begin to hope for recognition. I was present, with a great crowd of electrons, imprisoned within a glass globe from which the air had been extracted. We were very pleased to find that the surrounding space had been cleared of air, for it was apparent that the experimenter was going to make us jump across from one end of the glass tube to the other.

A crowd of us had collected on the extremity of a wire, or "electrode," at the one end of the tube, while another similar crowd was present on the other electrode at the opposite end of the tube. While I speak of a crowd, meaning that there were millions of us, I do not suggest that we were overcrowded, for we had plenty of elbow-room to move about on the atoms to which we were attached. All in a moment the scene was changed. We felt a crowd of electrons pressing us forward and forcing us right up to the very end of the electrode. We found that the crowd was approaching by a wire leading into the tube. Soon the crowding had reached such a condition that we became alarmed; we could see no way of escape. We were imprisoned by the glass walls, but we soon discovered that many of the electrons who had been stationed on the other electrode had deserted their posts and fled along a wire leading out of the tube. If we could only follow them. It would be a tremendous jump to get over to the other wire, but the way was fairly clear of air. When the overcrowding reached a certain point we were literally shot across from the one electrode to the other. This was the first time I had ever experienced anything of the kind, but many fellow-electrons had gone through similar performances for years at the hands of other experimenters.

However, it was somewhat alarming to be fired off like a rocket across the tube. What happened after that I cannot recollect, but some time later I was present in that or a similar tube when I heard the experimenter say to a friend that he believed there were particles flying across his tube. We sent news all along the line stating that at last we had been discovered, and I can assure you that we felt proud. But our joy was not long-lived, for it turned out that we were considered to be particles or atoms of matter; the experimenter spoke of us as "radiant matter." This was a real disappointment.

It took us some time to recover from our disappointment at being mistaken for clumsy atoms of matter. We are of a higher order of things altogether. No atom of matter can travel at speeds such as we can. We cross these vacuum tubes with speeds equal to millions of miles per minute.

A great many of us were kept busy within vacuum tubes by other experimenters, but nothing very exciting happened. Indeed, we had lost all hope of attracting man's attention to ourselves as long as we were imprisoned within these tubes. In the meantime our hopes were revived by news which reached us from another quarter.

We heard that a very learned man had declared boldly that there did exist little particles which revolved around the atoms of matter, and that it was the motion of these tiny particles in the æther which produced the well-known waves of *light*. There was considerable rejoicing among us, for we were anxious to have our services recognised by man. This great man was not guessing merely; he was willing to prove by mathematical calculations that we did exist in reality. Of course, we ourselves required no proof of our existence, but we believed that man would be convinced. Our high hopes were soon laid low; news reached us that people were shaking their heads and saying that figures could be made to prove anything.

After we had settled down to our ordinary duties, we got word that at last man had really detected us in a flame of gas. This seemed quite reasonable, for, as I shall relate to you in another chapter, we have a very lively time of it in a flame of gas. However, when we were informed that man had discovered us by means of a sort of telescope arrangement, I, for one, began to doubt the truth of the discovery. Some time before this I had heard that men were spying at gas flames in the hope of finding us, and this seemed most ridiculous, for if man could not see the large congregations of us called *atoms*, how could he expect to see individual electrons? My ignorance was dispelled when it was explained that man had not been looking for us directly, but for the æther waves which we produce. But I have not had an opportunity of explaining to you how some of us produce waves in the æther; I shall have to wait till a later chapter. In the meantime I may say that since this important discovery I have taken some part in an experiment similar to the historic one wherein we were detected, but of that too I shall have more to say again.

The rejoicing at this discovery was not confined to us, for men of science were quick to grasp the importance which was attached to this new knowledge. We felt that man was bound to acknowledge our services from that day. The next event was our christening, and this was not all plain sailing. Indeed, we have been rather annoyed with one name which some good friends persist in giving us. I refer to the name *corpuscle*, which we feel to be a sort of nickname, although it may have been suggested in all kindness. It may be difficult for you to appreciate our dislike to this name, but it seems to us to savour too much of material things. It is not dignified; you must remember we are not matter. We are delighted with what we prefer to call our real name—electron—for that speaks of electricity. As you know, we are units of particles of negative electricity, and so this seems a most sensible and suitable name. But I must hasten to tell of some of our everyday duties in which we serve man.

CHAPTER VII
A STEADY MARCH

The Electron explains how they produce the electric current. How man discovered means of making the electrons march. A simple explanation of how a complete electric circuit is always necessary. How an "earth circuit" works. How the marching electrons can do work

THE SCRIBE'S NOTE ON CHAPTER SEVEN

The steady motion of electrons from atom to atom along a wire, or other conductor, constitutes the well-known "electric current."

The moving electrons disturb the æther around the wire and produce what we know as a "magnetic field."

The electron explains why it is necessary to have a complete circuit before any electric current can take place.

Also how one length of wire may be used to connect two distant places provided the two extremities of the wire are buried in the earth.

Personally I knew nothing about marching until quite recently. Indeed, none of my fellow-electrons seem to have had definite ideas of regular marches previous to last century. That century is prominent in our history as well as in man's. There is no doubt that before then we must have made more or less regular marches through the crust of the earth and elsewhere; but for myself I have no such recollection previous to the following occasion.

The experience was not a very exciting one. I found myself passing along from atom to atom in a copper wire. But what was of special interest to us was that it became evident that these enforced marches were being deliberately controlled by man. Of course you will understand that man knew nothing of our existence at that time. All he knew was that when he placed a piece of zinc and a piece of copper in a chemical solution, there were certain effects produced in some mysterious fashion. For instance, when he connected the top of the two metals in this chemical cell or "battery" by a piece of wire, he got what he described as an *electric current*. Now all that happened really was this. The chemical action in this battery which man had devised caused a rearrangement among the atoms composing the metals and the solution, with the result that we poor electrons had to rearrange our domiciles. As an accumulation of electrons gathered on the zinc, some of us were forced along the connecting wire towards the copper. As long as the chemical action in the battery was kept up, so long were we kept on the march from the zinc to the copper by way of the wire.

Man tried increasing the length of this wire bridge across which we had to pass, but we had no difficulty in making our way along. But you must not run away with the idea that we rush along the wire with lightning speed. Although we can fly through the æther at a prodigious speed, our progress from atom to atom in a wire is more like a snail-pace. As a matter of fact, our rate of march is much less than the walking pace of a man; indeed it may be stated conveniently as so many yards per hour.

Some people may find it difficult to believe that our rate of march is so very slow. Their front door is a good many yards away from their electric bell, but it does not take us an hour, or any appreciable part of a minute, to summon the maid. The secret is that there is a whole regiment of us along the wire, and before one of us moves on to a neighbouring atom, another electron must move off that atom and on to its neighbour, and so on. In this way the electrons at the far end of the wire commence to move at practically the same moment as those near the battery.

It has been a source of amusement to me to see people perfectly mystified by the fact that they can get no electric current unless they have a complete circuit. What else could they expect? How could man march if he had no road to march on? You see, the reason for our march is that we wish to escape from the over-crowding on the zinc, and we are forced towards the copper. The atoms composing the wire are our stepping-stones, and if there is not a complete chain of atoms we are helpless. You have already heard how we can jump an air-space under very great pressure, but that condition does not exist in the present case. When we are disturbed by the chemical action of the battery, we should prefer to have a short-cut from the zinc to the copper, but if the only path man gives us is by way of a long wire, then we must be content to travel that road, in order to reach the copper. It is a matter of little moment to us what arrangement man makes as long as he gives us a complete path. For instance, he may lead us out from the zinc to a distant telegraph instrument, and then, instead of providing a second wire to take us back to the battery, he may conduct us by a short wire to the earth. We are quite content to lose ourselves in this great reservoir, provided man places another short wire from the earth to the copper of the battery at the other end of the line. Then as we slip off at the one end of the line, an equal number of electrons can climb up at the other end, and thus enable all our friends in the long wire to keep up a steady march.

This march of ours is not merely a means of transporting ourselves from one place to another; it is to enable us to do work. It is only when we are in motion that we can do useful work, for we must move before we can disturb the æther, and it is by means of the æther that we transmit energy.

If you place a magnetic needle or mariner's compass near a wire along which we are making a steady march, you will find that we can affect our fellow-electrons who are stationed within the magnetic needle. We cause the needle to swing round and take up a position at right angles to our line of march. We succeed in doing this because these electrons in the magnetic needle are on the move also. But this reminds me that I have never told you how we produce that æther disturbance which you call *magnetism*.

When, as children, you played with toy magnets in the nursery, little did you think that there was a host of tiny electrons amusing you. And yet we electrons are responsible entirely for all magnetic effects, as I shall proceed to explain.

CHAPTER VIII

A USEFUL DANCE

A perpetual dance. A responsible position. How the safety of the mariner depends upon the electrons' dance. How electrons produce a magnet. A convenient kind of magnet, which gains and loses its attractive power when desired. How a permanent magnet is made. The great service of electrons in modern life

THE SCRIBE'S NOTE ON CHAPTER EIGHT

We believe magnetism to be due to electrons revolving around atoms of iron and other magnetic substances, as related by the electron in this chapter.

We have seen that the steady motion of electrons along a wire produces a magnetic field around the wire.

Therefore if we have electrons revolving round and round the atoms in a piece of iron, there will be a miniature magnetic field around each atom.

The electron explains why a piece of iron does not show the magnetic power locked up within it until it is "magnetised."

The electron refers to electro-magnets; an electro-magnet is simply a piece of soft iron with a coil of insulated wire wound around it.

The iron only shows its magnetic power as long as a current of electricity is kept passing through the surrounding coil of wire, for reasons which the electron explains.

I may tell you quite frankly that I have never taken part in the perpetual dance of which I am about to tell you. I am of a free and roaming disposition, but I have often watched some of my fellow-electrons at this work. Of course, it is pleasant work, as all our duties are, now that man acknowledges our services.

We are responsible for the behaviour of the mariner's compass needle. It is we who cause it to point continually in one definite direction. If we ceased to dance around the iron atoms in the compass needle aboard a ship, the man at the helm could not tell in what direction he was going, and sooner or later he would be almost certain to wreck his vessel. For this service alone man ought to be grateful to us, but before I have finished my story, you will find that even this important duty is but a small affair when compared with many of our other tasks.

There is one matter I should like to make quite clear to you. Although we electrons are all identical, we have different stations to fill. You have doubtless become familiar with my roving disposition, and you probably think of me as a detachable electron. Then there are our friends who are locked up within the atoms of matter—part and parcel of the atom. And now I am introducing you to those electrons who act as satellites to the atoms, revolving around them at a comparatively great distance, just as the moon revolves around the earth. These are the electrons which give rise to the magnetism in a piece of iron. There are other electrons which perform very rapid revolutions around all classes of atoms, but I shall introduce these friends later on.

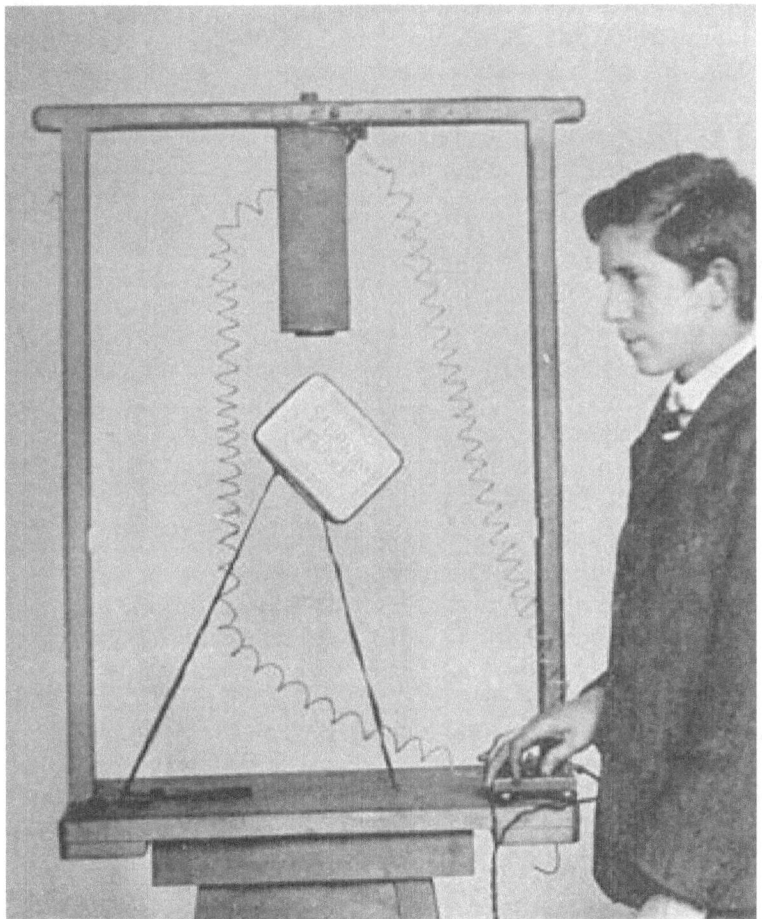

A Tobacco-Tin Defying Gravitation

That phenomenon known as "magnetism" is due to the steady locomotion of electrons, as explained in the text. Here we see a large magnet attracting a tinned iron box which is tethered to the table by two cords. The result is that the box is supported in the air. The spiral wires are connected to the electro-magnet, an explanation of which is given in Chapter VIII.

I need hardly remark that a piece of ordinary iron does not behave like a magnet. Indeed, it is fortunate that it does not. If it did, man could not get along with his work very well. The hammer would stick to the head of the nail it had struck, the fire-irons would stick to the fender, while the cook's pots and pans would hold on to the kitchen range. That would be a very stupid arrangement, but we electrons have really no say in the matter of arrangement. We are always on the move, performing a perpetual dance around the iron atoms, but the atoms arrange themselves in a higgledy-piggledy fashion, so that the electrons on one atom pull the æther in one direction while others pull the æther in an opposite direction. In this way the outward effect is not perceptible. When, however, man places a coil of wire around the iron, and makes a crowd of electrons march along the wire, these marching electrons affect the æther, which in turn influences the satellite electrons which are revolving around the atoms of iron. You may be somewhat surprised when I tell you that, owing to this æther disturbance, these satellite electrons are able to produce a rearrangement among the atoms. If you doubt my word, you may easily prove the truth of the statement. If you magnetise a long bar of iron you will find that its length is actually altered. This is due to our having disturbed the arrangement of the atoms.

Perhaps I should explain that when we force the atoms into their new condition, we can do so only under the æther stress set up by our fellow-electrons who are marching in the neighbouring wire. Whenever their march ceases the æther stress is withdrawn, and the atoms are able to fall back into their old higgledy-piggledy condition. In this way man is able to make a piece of iron a magnet and to unmake it as often as he cares by simply switching on and off the electric current from the wire surrounding the iron.

If a piece of hard steel is used in place of soft iron, then we find that the atoms are not so easily disturbed, but when they are once brought into line with one another, they will remain in their new condition after the æther disturbance has been withdrawn. It may seem strange to you that quite a small percentage of carbon atoms added to the pure soft iron should cause such a marked difference, but the matter seems plain enough to us. Man was so impressed with the manner in which the atoms were evidently fixed in their new condition that he spoke of *permanent magnets*. It is especially fortunate for man that these pieces of steel do retain their magnetism, and give us a reliable mariner's compass. But I shall tell you how you may disturb even these sedate atoms. If you hammer the metal very vigorously, or if you heat it to redness, you will find that the atoms have been freed from what appeared to be their permanent position, and they are back to their old higgledy-piggledy condition, so that we electrons are all opposing one another. Remember we are hard at work all the time although we may be giving no outward sign of our activity.

While we render an important aid to man by providing this permanent magnet for his compass, you will find that a very great deal of our assistance to man in his everyday life depends upon our behaviour in soft iron electro-magnets. It is in these that man can control our behaviour at will. It is through this simple piece of apparatus—the electro-magnet—that man has been able to accomplish so much in signalling to his friends at a distance. It is also by means of these electro-magnets that man can get us to turn an electric motor, and so on. But I must tell you, first of all, how we enable man to signal to a distance, or, in other words, how we carry man's news.

CHAPTER IX

HOW WE CARRY MAN'S NEWS

The method of sending the news. The Electron's personal experience.
A series of forced marches. How man controls the electrons. How
the electrons reproduce the signals

THE SCRIBE'S NOTE ON CHAPTER NINE

The electron explains wherein its method differs from all other methods.

It is well known that within recent years the old iron telegraph wires have been replaced by much lighter copper wires; the electron explains the reason for this change.

It describes how the electrons manage to work the most widely used form of telegraph instrument, which is called the "Morse," after its inventor.

Here we find one of the practical applications of the electro-magnet described in the preceding chapter.

It is we electrons who have so very far outdistanced all material carriers of news. You must acknowledge that the best runner, the swiftest horse, the fastest express train, and the prize carrier pigeon, are all nowhere when compared with us electrons.

But I do not wish to mislead you in any way, and I can speak from personal experience in this case. We do not race off with man's messages in the same sense as these other messengers do. Our swiftness of communication depends upon the simple fact that man provides a whole connecting regiment of us between the two distant places. And when the order to march is given we all move off at practically the same moment. In this way the electrons at the far end of the connecting wire are able to cause signals there immediately. This is the secret of man's success in being able to hold immediate communication with his distant friends. His success is due entirely to the co-operation of us electrons.

My personal experience has been in connection with a very simple telegraphic arrangement. Indeed, the most of our duties in transmitting messages are performed with this particular kind of instrument, known as a "Morse sounder."

At the time of which I speak, I had become attached to an atom of iron in the end of a long telegraph wire. From this you will probably guess that my experience was gained some time ago, for man does not use iron wires nowadays in fitting up telegraph lines. He used iron at first, and some of these lines still exist, but when he discovered that a very much lighter copper wire would serve the same purpose, he discarded the heavy iron wires. Man explained the matter by saying that the copper offered less resistance to the electric current, and the majority of people were quite satisfied with this kind of explanation. Of course these are merely convenient phrases which give man no real reason for the difference. The real reason is that we electrons are able to move about from one copper atom to another with very much greater ease than we can among the iron atoms. That is the reason why man made the change from iron to copper wires, although he had no idea of the reason at the time.

To return to my experience in connection with a telegraph instrument, I found that we were being subjected to a series of forced marches. The whole regiment of electrons along the line made a forward move. The line of march ended in a short length of fine wire wound around a piece of soft iron to form an electro-magnet. The end of the wire dipped into the earth, as I have explained in an earlier chapter.

Now all that we electrons had to do was to make a forward move, halt, forward again, another halt, and so on. Sometimes the signal to halt was longer in being given than at other times, but we found that this was intentional, and that there were two definite lengths of march. I have explained already how we marching electrons cause an electro-magnet to attract a piece of iron and let it go again as soon as we cease marching. It only remains for me to give you a general statement of how we work the Morse telegraph.

Man has arranged a little lever with an iron end-piece immediately above the electro-magnet, so that the magnet may attract it. Of course you are aware that it is the electrons within the soft-iron core of the electro-magnet who produce the magnetic effect. Every time we electrons in the surrounding wire make a forward move, the electro-magnet pulls down the end of the little lever referred to. As long as we keep marching, so long will the end of the lever remain down, but the moment we halt, the lever is free to be pulled up by a spring attached to it. The movements of the lever indicate the length of our long and short marches, and it is by means of these that man sends signals. All that he does is to control our march, by means of an electric push and a battery at one end of the wire, and it is we who produce the signals at the distant end of the wire. Each time man presses the push we move the distant lever. When we pull the lever down it is so arranged that it makes a sound like "click," and when we let it spring up against a stop it makes another sound not unlike "clack." Our long and short marches are therefore converted into long and short "click-clacks." Man has made a simple code of signals representing his alphabet, and right merrily do we rap out the signals for which we receive orders at the distant end of the wire, while some one at the other end listens to the sounds we cause to be made.

I have told you enough of our duties to let you see how we are able to carry man's news from one part of the earth to any other part. By far the greatest part of our signalling work is done with this simple Morse sounder.

It may interest you to note that we can produce those signals far faster than man can read them. When man found this out he took advantage of our powers.

He made an automatic transmitter which could manipulate the make-and-break of the battery current far more rapidly than any human fingers could do. Then as we rapped off the signals with lightning speed at the distant end, he attached a little ink-wheel to the end of the moving lever, so that it could mark short and long strokes on a ribbon of paper passing close to it. Although man could not distinguish the signals by his ear he was able to read the record of those we caused to be left upon the paper ribbon.

We have been made to work many other forms of telegraph instruments. In some of these we control type-letters, while in others we imitate handwriting, but all these are merely adaptations of our powers of marching. We are proud of our achievements in rapid signalling, which all right-thinking people have not been slow to acknowledge.

CHAPTER X

HOW WE COMMUNICATE WITH DISTANT SHIPS

An entirely different means of communication. A surprise to man, but not to the electrons. How the electrons produce waves in the surrounding æther. How these waves disturb distant electrons. The Electron's personal experience. Its description of its actions in a wireless telegraph station

THE SCRIBE'S NOTE ON CHAPTER TEN

In this chapter the electron deals with that modern marvel—*Wireless Telegraphy*.

Here the æther of space plays a very prominent part.

The author has given some particulars about the æther in the first chapter (*What the Story is about*).

In conjunction with that, the electron may be left to tell its own story.

Our duties in this case are totally different from those of which I have been telling you. While we electrons can do many wonderful things, we cannot march through space. We may be fired off like bullets from the sun to the earth, but that is quite another matter. I shall have something to say about that fact later on. You have seen already that man can make us jump only a very short distance, even when he has cleared our path of the obstructing air, as he does in a vacuum tube.

If men were to provide us with a complete path of metal atoms from the shore to the ship, we could set to work upon the simple plan which I have described in the preceding chapter. But, needless to say, man has more sense than to attempt to keep up metallic connection with a ship going away out to sea.

Even the wisest men were surprised when they heard that we electrons could signal through space to great distances without any connecting wires. We ourselves were not surprised. Had we not been doing this very thing from the foundation of the world? Our fellow-electrons in the sun have never ceased to communicate with those of us upon the earth. Of course I am referring at present to those æther waves which man calls *heat* and *light*. But the waves which we make to carry man's messages through space are of the very same nature, the only difference being that they are much longer, or, in other words, much farther apart. They do not follow each other so closely, and they do not affect the eye or the sense of touch. However, these long waves are able to bestir some of us electrons who are situated at a great distance from the sending electrons.

Our method of producing such waves in the æther is by surging to and fro from atom to atom in an upright wire. When we make a rapid to-and-fro motion we send out great waves in the æther. The original plan adopted by man was to make us jump across a spark-gap, but in this case also it was our rapid oscillation to and fro that produced the waves. If we wish the waves to carry to a great distance, we must club together in considerable force to supply the necessary energy. The energy which we can get from a battery and induction coil is not sufficient for any very long distances. In such cases we require the aid of a *dynamo*, a machine about which I shall have some experience to relate in another chapter.

In communicating through space, our position is very similar to that of two men shouting to one another over a distance. The one man disturbs the air, thus sending air-waves (sound) over to his friend, and these waves produce certain sensations which he can interpret. I should like you to understand that we electrons are upon a higher plane than atoms of matter. We cause waves in the all-pervading æther, not among clumsy particles of air. After these æther waves have travelled enormous distances they retain sufficient energy to disturb electrons situated at the distant place.

I shall tell you of the first experience I had in this connection. I found myself attached to an atom of *nickel*, a kind of atom which looks to us electrons very much like an iron atom, because it has nearly the same number of electrons composing it, only they are arranged differently. But I was telling you that I found myself on this nickel atom sealed up in a small glass tube. Of course there were myriads of similar atoms all around me, but I did not feel very happy. I was being urged forward, and yet I could not get across from some atoms to others, for the nickel was in the form of loose filings. From past experience I knew that there was a battery along the line somewhere; I could feel the strain. All of a sudden I was startled to find that I could move forward. Exactly what happened, I am not at liberty to tell, but this much I may say, that it was the arrival of some æther waves which altered the condition of things among the filings in the tube.

A Motor-Car with Wireless Telegraph

It has become quite a fashion in America to have motor-cars fitted up for wireless telegraphy. That the electrons play an important part in telegraphing through space is explained fully in Chapter X.

We had just started out on our march forward when we received such a shaking that we found ourselves in the same isolated positions as at first; we could not get across from one particle to another. More æther waves arrived, we made a fresh start, then came another rude shaking, and so on we went starting and stopping. Indeed, it was the regularity of these long and short marches that gave me the first idea that we were being controlled by some telegraph operator. We were amused to find that the rude shaking, of which I have been telling you, was caused by the action of some of our fellow-electrons. Some of them in their march around an electro-magnet in the receiving instrument caused a little lever to knock against our tube and give us a sudden jolt.

I should like you to notice that the energy with which we moved the telegraph instrument did not come from the distant station. It was a local battery which worked the receiving instrument, but this battery was controlled by the incoming æther waves affecting the tube of filings. There is really no mystery about the matter, but I am anxious not to take credit for anything more wonderful than we have actually accomplished.

We electrons have rendered a very great service to man by enabling him to communicate with his friends who are far out on the ocean, and cut off from all possible chance of material communication. We are willing to serve man on land also, though we very much prefer the ordinary marching arrangement if he will provide a connecting wire. The fact is that we find it very much more difficult to send æther waves over land than we do over water.

I have heard some men ask how many different telegraph instruments may be worked at one place simultaneously without confusion. That is a question for man himself to answer. We electrons are able to produce any variety of waves of different frequency or length; it remains only for man to construct apparatus that will respond only to a definite rate of waves. I hear that man has made considerable progress in tuning the wireless instruments.

Some men are eager to get us to carry messages through space across the great oceans from shore to shore. We shall not refuse, provided man supplies sufficient energy, but I must admit that we electrons prefer the submarine cable. Of course man may put this down to our laziness; we certainly prefer as little severe straining as possible.

I have been telling you of my earliest and only personal experience in connection with space telegraphy. I understand that greatly improved methods have been adopted since that time, but I have never happened to drift in their direction.

CHAPTER XI
HOW WE REPRODUCE SPEECH

Why it is not correct to speak of the electrons as carriers of speech. The action of electrons in the working of telephones. The Electron's own experience in wireless telephony

THE SCRIBE'S NOTE ON CHAPTER ELEVEN

In the first part of this chapter the electron explains the part it plays in ordinary telephony.

The reader will picture the transmitting instrument at the one end of the line influencing the receiving instrument at the distant end.

Towards the end of the chapter the electron turns its attention to the newer subject of *wireless telephony*, which has been accomplished now over a distance of several hundred miles.

My scribe suggested a rather clumsy title for this chapter—"Electrons *versus* atoms as carriers of speech." I expect he made this suggestion without much thought, for there are two serious objections to such a title.

In the first place, we are not carriers of speech. We are controlled by speech at one end of the telephone line, and we make a reproduction of the speech at the distant end of the line. No sound passes between the two places; there is only a movement of electrons along the connecting line.

My second objection to the hurriedly suggested title is that it is hardly fair to make any comparison between the achievements of atoms of matter and those of ourselves. We are not in the same category as atoms. Besides, we electrons are dependent entirely upon the material atoms for making our work useful to man. For instance, we might keep on making waves in the æther for all time, and yet if the atoms of matter were to pay no heed to those imperceptible waves, man would never be aware of their presence. Indeed we electrons act solely as go-betweens. On the other hand, it is only fair to ourselves to point out that a group of atoms in one town could never communicate with a group of atoms in a distant town unless we electrons came to their aid. It is true that over a very short distance the atoms may communicate directly. For instance, if a heavy blow is given to a large gong, the atoms of metal may vibrate so energetically that they succeed in disturbing the atoms of gas of the surrounding atmosphere for some considerable distance. But in the case of speech, the speaker cannot supply any great energy, so that he can disturb the atmosphere only to a very limited distance. We electrons, however, can do yeoman service in this respect. We have enabled men to speak to one another over immense distances.

The whole affair is very simple. Man speaks and causes the atmospheric atoms to vibrate and impinge upon a light disc or diaphragm in a simple instrument which man has named the *telephone*. This vibrating disc presses upon a myriad of carbon particles contained in a small case or box, the disc forming one side of the box. When these carbon particles are pressed together we electrons can get across more easily from atom to atom. There is a battery urging us forward, but our motion is dependent entirely upon the manner in which the vibrating disc presses upon the carbon particles. I cannot describe our movement in the line-wire as a march; it is in reality a surging to and fro.

You will understand that this to-and-fro motion of the electrons in the line-wire varies according to the vibrations of the sending disc, which is controlled by the speaker's voice. At the distant end of the line we electrons bring our magnetic powers into action. We keep varying the attractive powers of an electro-magnet, according to the motion of the electrons in the wire. This ever-changing magnet produces vibrations in an iron disc which is fixed close to the magnet. This disc is set vibrating in exact sympathy with the sending disc. When the listener places this receiving disc close to his ear, the vibrations are carried by the atmospheric atoms to his hearing apparatus. All that we electrons have done is to cause one disc to vibrate in exact synchrony with another distant disc. But that is all that is required, for the receiving disc will reproduce similar air-vibrations to those set up by the man's voice at the distant place. I have pointed out already that we do not attempt to carry the sound. It is true that the atoms of matter do the hard work, but it is we electrons who enable a group of atoms in one town to communicate with a group of atoms in a distant town.

It was natural that as soon as man found that he could work his telegraph instruments without the aid of connecting wires, he should try to do the same with his telephone instruments. We were sorry when we found men trying to use the original spark-telegraphy methods for telephones. While we had no difficulty in operating a telegraph instrument by means of æther waves and the tube of filings, it was quite impossible for us to produce telephone vibrations on the same principle. This spark method was a too rough-and-ready plan. The waves we produced were like sudden splashes in the æther ocean, whereas we knew that we must produce regular trains of continuous waves in order to reproduce telephone vibrations. However, you may be aware that we have succeeded by a different arrangement of apparatus. Indeed it may interest you to know that one of my most recent experiences has been in connection with some wireless-telephone experiments.

Unfortunately I was not in a very favourable position to learn all that was going on, but it was quite exciting work. I happened to be attached to an atom of copper in a length of wire which had been run up into the air on a sort of flag-pole arrangement. I need hardly say that I was not alone, for by this time you will have become accustomed to picture myriads of electrons occupying a very small space.

We were set vibrating to and fro with tremendous energy, but what bothered me most was the great variation in our movements. It was the nature of these variations which gave me the clue that we were being controlled by the vibrations of a telephone disc. I can tell you we did make a complex series of waves in the surrounding æther! These waves went out through space and influenced some electrons stationed at a great distance. When these electrons at the receiving station were set in motion they controlled the electric current from a local battery which set a second telephone disc vibrating in synchrony with the one at the sending station.

On questioning some of my fellow-electrons who happened to have been nearer the transmitting part of the instrument than I had been, I got some interesting information. They tell me that there was a dynamo and an arc lamp in our circuit, while the telephone instrument was in a neighbouring circuit. The electrons surging to and fro in the telephone circuit influenced those energetic electrons in the arc-lamp circuit to which the ærial wire was attached. You see that my position in the ærial wire was not a very advantageous one for observing what was taking place.

This was truly a great achievement—to enable one man to speak to another distant hundreds of miles, and without the aid of any connecting wire. I think you will agree with me that we have excelled all past records in the world of wonders.

CHAPTER XII
OUR HEAVIEST DUTIES

A roving commission. How electrons can move gigantic cars and trains. The action of electrons in dynamos and motors. How the electrons transmit the energy. What makes the motor go

THE SCRIBE'S NOTE ON CHAPTER TWELVE

Here the electron explains its behaviour in a dynamo at work.

The principle of the dynamo was discovered by Faraday in the thirties of last century.

He found that when a coil of wire was moved through a magnetic field, there was a current of electricity induced in the moving coil.

Experimental machines were constructed, and after a while a practical dynamo was evolved.

Wires are attached to a dynamo and the electric current is led out.

This current may be conducted to a distant tramway car, and, by sending the current through an electric motor, mechanical motion is produced and the car propelled along.

An electric motor is practically the same as a dynamo, but instead of turning its coil round in order to produce an electric current, we pass a current into the coil and it moves round. It will be sufficient to leave the electron to tell its own story.

This is another of those roving commissions in which I have been privileged to take part on more than one occasion.

If you think of the giant size of an electric tramway car or a railway train, and try to compare one of these with an electron, such as your humble servant, it will seem quite ridiculous that I should suggest that it is we electrons who move those huge vehicles. Yet such is the actual case.

Of course we require the application of very considerable power to urge us to so heavy a task. All the energy which we can get from a few electric batteries might enable us to drive a toy car, but when it comes to turning the wheels of a real car or train, we require a correspondingly greater amount of energy.

I may as well tell you quite frankly that we electrons are only the intermediaries or go-betweens. Indeed, you must have noticed that in every case we act merely as a connecting link between matter and the æther, and between the æther and matter.

But what I want to tell you of, is the part we play in moving an electric car or railway train. It is really all very simple if you could only see it from our standpoint. Picture a host of us attached to copper atoms in a coil of wire which is being moved through that disturbed æther called a *magnetic field*. We are set in motion immediately. It is true that when we are moved forward into the field we march off in one direction, only to be arrested and made to move off in the opposite direction as we leave the field, but it really makes no difference in our working capabilities as long as we are kept on the move. This is what is actually taking place in the armature of a dynamo as it revolves between the poles of the electro-magnet. There is no peace for us so long as the coil is kept revolving; we are kept in a constant state of rapid to-and-fro motion.

By permission of Siemens Schuckert Werke   *Berlin*

A Train Impelled by Moving Electrons

It is remarkable that the motion of electrons in an electric conductor can result in the movement of heavy vehicles. How this comes about is explained in Chapter XII.

This is all we electrons do in a dynamo, but when the ends of the outer circuit or mains are brought into contact with the ends of our revolving coil, we set the electrons in the mains surging to and fro in step with ourselves. Man describes this motion of the electrons in the mains as an *alternating electric current*, but by a simple commutator on the dynamo he may arrange that we set the electrons marching in one direction in the mains. This he describes as a *direct electric current*.

It is a matter of indifference to us whether man drives our coil round by means of a steam-engine, a water-wheel, or a wind-mill; all that we electrons want is to be kept surging or vibrating to and fro. Now you will be able to appreciate how we electrons get up sufficient motion to enable us to perform what I have described as *our heaviest duties*.

Perhaps you will find it difficult to believe me when I tell you that as we march along the connecting wire to a distant tramway car we transmit the energy through the surrounding æther, and not through the wire. This is our mode of working in every case, whether it be an electric bell, a telegraph, or telephone. That is to say, while we electrons move from atom to atom in the connecting wire, it is the disturbed æther surrounding us which transmits the energy. You must have realised by this time how very intimate is the relationship between ourselves and the æther.

To return to the tale of our tramway work, you will picture my fellow-electrons aboard the car being energised by the incoming current. Those electrons present in the armature coil of the motor are set into motion, as also are those in the wire of the neighbouring electro-magnet. The result is that these two sets of electrons so disturb the æther and affect one another that the coil is moved round into a different position. You will remember the experiment of which I told you, in which a magnetic needle would insist always in taking up a position at right angles to a wire in which an electric current is passing. Well, when the motor coil has turned into its new position, we electrons receive an impulse from our friends in the line-wire which causes us to retrace our steps in the coil. This action of ours causes the coil to make a further movement in the same direction as at first. Again we change our direction of march, and again the coil changes its position towards the electro-magnet. The sole duty of these electrons in the armature coil is to keep surging to and fro, while those electrons in the electro-magnet keep up a steady march in one direction. This arrangement necessitates the armature coil to keep changing its position continually, and when we have the armature coil spinning round at a steady pace, it is easy for man to connect the armature to the axles of the tramway car and cause us to drive the wheels round.

I need hardly say that it makes no difference to us whether we are asked to drive a tramway car, a railway train, or a host of machines in a factory or workshop. All that we electrons in the motor require is to have sufficient energy passed along to us from our fellows in the distant dynamo. Again I admit frankly that the atoms of matter play a very important part in these our heaviest duties, but you will see that without our active assistance they could not transmit the necessary energy to a distant car or train.

CHAPTER XIII

A BOON TO MAN

A simple explanation of how the electrons produce light. How the
Electron provides a connecting link between matter and the æther.
How light reaches the earth from the sun. How the electrons pro-
duce that beautiful luminous effect which man calls an "Aurora."
How the earth has become a negatively charged body. How elec-
trons produce radiant heat. The difference between light and heat

THE SCRIBE'S NOTE ON CHAPTER THIRTEEN

While it has been known for a long time that *light* and *radiant heat* are merely
waves in the æther, it was not known until recently how these waves were produced.

The discovery of electrons has given us a reasonable solution of our difficulty.

The electron explains the actions of its fellows in this great work of producing
light and heat.

Incidentally the electron explains how they produce an aurora in the heavens,
and how it is that the earth has become a negatively electrified body.

Every living thing is dependent upon our activities. It is we electrons who
send out heat and light from the sun, and it is we who receive these on their arrival upon this planet. Our action in the matter is really very simple, but until man
discovered our existence, he was mystified considerably.

We were amused to hear man say that the atoms of incandescent matter in
the sun produced waves in the æther, and that when these æther waves fell upon
other atoms on this planet, these were set into a state of vibration, thus producing
heat and light. Now if man had only stopped to think, he would have seen how
ridiculous it was to speak of atoms of matter producing waves in the æther. He
ought to have known that atoms of matter cannot affect the æther, for it offers no
resistance to matter moving through it.

Man might have pictured himself riding on the back of this great planet, flying through space at a speed very similar to that of a rifle bullet, and yet even the
flimsy blanket of air surrounding the planet is not disturbed by the æther through
which it is rushing.

It is true that the atoms of matter play an important part in the origin of heat,
but the atoms in the sun could no more affect the atoms on the earth than could a

man on the earth push the moon about. It is the very intimate connection between us electrons and the all-pervading æther which enables our fellows in the sun to communicate with those of us upon this planet. Where would man be without us?

Protection Against a Discharge of Electrons

When a man is encased completely in an over-all made of flexible metallic gauze he is proof against shock due to a discharge of high-tension electricity. The part played by electrons in the case of electric shock is explained in Chapter IV.

I cannot understand wherein man should find any mystery in connection with this very simple action of ours. You will picture our distant fellow-electrons making very rapid revolutions around the atoms of matter to which they are attached as satellites. Just as the moon circles around the earth, so do we circle around our atoms, but at an enormously greater speed. Of course the whole length of our orbit is inconceivably small, and the speed of our revolutions is inconceivably great. It is our rapid motion through the æther which produces those waves known to man as radiant heat and light. Some one may ask how it is that we electrons can disturb the æther while the giant atoms cannot. The obvious answer is that we are not matter, but electricity; we are not in the same category as atoms of matter.

To complete the picture which I was drawing, you have only to think of the æther waves arriving upon this planet and disturbing sympathetic electrons, causing them to revolve around their atoms in similar fashion to our distant fellows who are producing the æther waves.

It may be that some people get confused between this action and that of those electrons who are shot off bodily from the sun towards the earth. Believe me, there is no connection between the two things. The stream of electrons shot off from the sun is deflected towards the magnetic poles of the earth, and as the electrons enter the upper layers of the atmosphere they produce that beautiful luminous effect which man describes as an *Aurora*.

I have never taken part in one of these great displays, for, as far as my recollection goes, I have never been in the sun, although some fellow-electrons declare that at one time we were all in the same great glowing mass of which the sun, and every member of the solar system, formed a part. However that may be, I certainly have no experience of auroræ, but I have assisted in producing the very same effect upon a small scale within a vacuum tube. The air remaining in these so-called vacuum tubes is just as rarified as the air in the upper layers of the atmosphere, and when we are shot across the tube we act in the same way as those electrons arriving upon this planet from the sun.

You will observe that as a surplus of electrons arrives upon the earth from the sun, the earth is naturally a negatively electrified body, but I need hardly say that the earth does not keep all the electrons which arrive upon it.

My scribe points out that I am wandering from the story which I set out to tell in this chapter, so I shall try and please him.

The direct cause of light, whether it be natural or artificial, is the rapid motion of electrons around atoms of matter. If they revolve at a comparatively slow speed they produce those æther waves which man calls *radiant heat*. If these satellite electrons, however, desire to affect the eye of man, they have to move around at a very much greater speed. If we travel at too fast a speed, then we cease to cause the sensation of light. But, believe me, all the waves we make are of the same nature, no matter what names man has given them. The only difference we can make in the waves is the rate at which they follow one another. Of course we can also make them larger or smaller in height, or, in other words, of greater or less amplitude, but that does not affect their properties.

In the following chapter I shall tell you of some remarkable phenomena which our different æther waves produce in the brain of man.

CHAPTER XIV
HOW WE PRODUCE COLOUR

What colour is really. How the different colour sensations are stimulated by the electrons. The Electron as a faithful satellite to the atom. How electrons can produce the different æther waves. How the electrons respond to the different waves. The production of artificial light. Co-operation of the electrons. Man's ridiculously wasteful processes. The electrons' secret

THE SCRIBE'S NOTE ON CHAPTER FOURTEEN

Colour is merely a sensation in the brain.

What the electrons really produce are æther waves, and these give rise to the sensations of colour.

However, the electrons may claim to produce colour in the same sense as we savages produce pain in fellow-men by firing rifle-bullets at them.

The electron explains how some objects appear white, while others are red, and so forth.

It explains also how electrons produce artificial light.

The electron twits man upon his ridiculously wasteful processes of obtaining artificial light.

In the preceding chapter I have been telling you how we electrons produce waves in the æther ocean. I pointed out that if we make the waves follow each other at too slow or too fast a rate they fail to affect man's eyes.

It may seem strange to you that only a very small range of our æther waves should affect man's visionary apparatus. Of course this limitation lies beyond our province; we can produce endless variety of æther waves—it is man's organs which fail to appreciate the bulk of these. However, there is plenty of variety in the sensations which we can produce in man. If we make the waves follow each other at a certain speed, man says he has the sensation of *red*. If we move faster, he speaks of *orange-colour*, and as we increase our speed he names his further sensations as *yellow*, *green*, *blue*, and *violet*. Then if we combine all these waves—that is, if we produce them all at one time—he says he has the sensation of *white*. If we produce none of these waves, he calls the result *black*.

While we electrons are very versatile, our actions are dependent in a great measure upon circumstances. For instance, if an electron is acting as a satellite to one particular kind of atom, its rate of revolution around that atom may be very different from that of an electron similarly attached to another kind of atom. We electrons are all identical, but the speed of revolution is determined by the kind of atom. The reason is very simple; electrons revolve around some atoms at a much greater distance than they would around other atoms. Those making only the smaller orbits not only get around their atoms in less time, but they are also travelling at a greater pace. It is this fact which enables the electrons to produce the various wave-lengths which stimulate the different colour sensations in the brain of man.

I think you will have no difficulty in seeing how it is that we come to produce such a variety of wave-lengths—in other words, how we are able to make the waves follow each other more or less rapidly. You will understand that we do not produce colours; we merely make various waves in the æther, and these waves excite the colour sensations in man. I mention this simple fact, because I hear many people speaking of our æther waves as "coloured rays," which, of course, is quite a ridiculous description.

Suppose some of those waves which give rise to the red sensation happen to fall upon a lump of matter which contains only electrons capable of producing waves that affect the green sensation. What will happen? There will be no response, and the object, although viewed by "red light," will appear black.

If an object, such as the white paper upon which my scribe is recording my story, contains a variety of atoms with electrons capable of revolving at all the different rates which produce colour sensations, then when "white light" falls upon the object it appears white (all the colour sensations combined). If, on the other hand, a "red light" only falls upon it, then only the electrons capable of responding to that rate of wave will be set in motion, and the object will appear red, and so on with the other rates of æther waves.

So far I have been telling you what happens when different waves of light fall upon us. Now I shall endeavour to explain how man has caused us to produce artificial light. At present all man's methods in this direction are dependent upon making some substance so hot that it becomes incandescent. Even his most modern methods seem to us to be ridiculously wasteful and most roundabout. I shall speak only of the electric glow lamp, as I have had some experience in connection with this.

On one occasion I had been taking part in a regular forward march from copper atom to copper atom in a conducting wire. I had no idea of the purpose of our march till I suddenly found myself handed over to some carbon atoms, who were in a very lively state of vibration. We had much more difficulty in making our way through this substance, and it was the passive resistance offered to the advance of the electrons who had preceded me that had driven the carbon atoms into this state of great excitement. In our march through the copper conductor we had been offered very little resistance, so that we had left the copper atoms in peace—at least man could not detect easily any excitement (heat). But so long as our forced march was maintained among the carbon atoms, so long did the high temperature exist.

You will understand I and the other marching electrons did not produce the waves of light sent out by the glow lamp. What we did was to set the atoms of carbon into a rapid vibratory state, and they in turn caused their satellite electrons to hasten their pace. Some electrons produced one rate of waves, and some another rate, but by the time the carbon was incandescent there were electrons sending out all the variety of wave-lengths, the combination of which produces the sensation of white.

I have accused man of adopting very wasteful processes, so I had better explain the matter. In the preceding description of what is occurring in an electric glow lamp, I have spoken only of those æther waves which constitute light. But there are myriads of electrons in the carbon of the glow lamp that never attain the requisite speed to produce those waves; they revolve around their atoms at too slow a rate. They certainly disturb the æther, but the crests of the waves are so far apart that they do not affect the eyes of man. The business of these waves is to set up heat in the bodies upon which they fall. You may be surprised to know that in this contrivance of man, called an electric glow lamp, and, indeed, in all his other artificial light-producers, he causes far more electrons to produce radiant heat than the desired light waves. A most wasteful process!

Man has a long way to travel yet before he succeeds in producing artificial light by a reasonable process. Indeed I doubt if any of you can realise, as we do, how exceedingly stupid the existing methods are. Think for a moment of the glow-worm, in which we electrons produce light without setting up any wasteful heat waves. There is a strong contrast between this peaceful plan and that of the excited carbon atoms. When will man succeed in discovering this secret of ours?

CHAPTER XV
WE SEND MESSAGES FROM THE STARS

The kind of messages referred to. How the electrons have informed man of what the stars are made. How man reads the electrons' wireless messages. How it is other electrons that enable man to read the messages. The real explanation of reflection of light. How light is absorbed by some objects. How some substances are transparent. Why objects appear coloured. What makes the lines in the spectra of stars. The spectroscope

THE SCRIBE'S NOTE ON CHAPTER FIFTEEN

It is remarkable that man has been able to discover what the distant stars are made of.

Our knowledge concerning the chemistry of the stars has been obtained by means of the spectroscope, in which a beam of light from the star is passed through a glass prism.

The result is the well-known image of the coloured spectrum, in which certain well-defined lines appear, according to the distant elements originating the æther waves.

The electron explains the whole subject from its own point of view.

It is only within recent times that man has observed that we send messages from the distant stars to this planet. But there is nothing new to us in this proceeding; we have been busy sending these messages ever since the solar system was formed. Through all those ages we have kept on sending these messages, knowing that in time man must come to take notice of them.

If the subject should happen to be new to you, you will be anxious to know to what kind of messages I refer. Needless to say, they are wireless messages—waves in the great æther ocean. The waves, to which I refer specially, fall within that small range of which I told you something in the preceding chapter. In other words, they are those waves to which man has given the name *light*. But what special information do these waves, coming from the stars, convey to man? They tell him of what materials these distant stars are made. Needless to say, it is we electrons who produce those informative waves.

You are familiar with our method of producing waves. You know that we whirl around the atoms of matter at prodigious speeds, and that according to the number of revolutions we make per second, we produce waves of corresponding frequencies.

In an earlier chapter I have hinted that the speed of the revolving electron is determined by the kind of atom to which it acts as a satellite. For instance, when electrons revolve around iron atoms they produce certain wave-lengths, while those moving around hydrogen atoms produce an entirely different series of waves. But how is man to recognise these?

It is quite evident that man may gaze at a distant star and be little the wiser concerning the different lengths of the waves which impinge upon his eyes. He may observe that the sensation is inclined to red, from which he may infer that the waves are long ones—that they are farther apart than some of the waves produced by a white-hot body. But had man been content to try and decipher our wireless messages in this rough-and-ready manner, he would never have gained the interesting information which we have now placed in his hands. How, then, did we enable man to read our messages?

Our plan may seem to be somewhat mysterious, but I assure you that it is really very simple. When these æther waves of light fall upon a triangular prism of glass, the waves are bent out of their normally straight path. But the point that may seem strange to you, is that those waves which produce the sensation of red are not bent so much as the others. The more rapidly the waves follow one another, the greater is the bending of such a ray from its original direction. In this way the various wave-lengths are all spread out, so that they form an image like a coloured ribbon, red at one end, being followed by orange, yellow, green, blue, and violet. Every man must be familiar with this coloured spectrum. When some of my fellows are enclosed in drops of water in the air they produce a great rainbow spectrum across the heavens. But I must tell you how we electrons succeed in bending these rays of light.

I have told you already how we either absorb or reflect the æther waves which happen to fall upon us. In most substances it is only those electrons very near the surface that are disturbed. They succeed in stopping the waves. They may do this in either of two different ways. If the satellite electrons are attracted strongly by their atoms, the electrons will spin around the atoms keeping time to the movements of the incoming waves, and in this way the electrons take up the energy of the waves. In doing this, the electrons send out fresh waves in the æther. This is the real explanation of what man calls *reflection* of light.

The Spectroscope and the Electrons' Wireless Messages

The spectroscope is seen in the extreme left of No. 1 photograph. The instrument is explained at page 207.

The operator is passing an electric current through a glass tube containing a rarefied gas, causing the gas to become luminous. When he examines its light through the spectroscope he sees bright lines as shown in photograph No. 2, and from the position of these lines he can tell what substance is producing the light. No. 2 is the spectrum of mercury vapour. No. 3 is part of the spectrum of the sun. Note the dark lines, as explained in the text.

In the second case, the electrons are not so firmly attached to their atoms, so that the incoming waves dislodge them, and they are knocked about from atom to atom, and in this way the energy of the waves is frittered away. Man speaks of the light having been *absorbed* by the substance upon which it fell. In both cases the only electrons which take part in these actions are those electrons who can move in sympathy with the incoming waves.

It will be clear to you that only those of us who are near the surface of a substance know anything about these incoming waves. The electrons attached to atoms in the interior of the substance are left in peace, owing to the defensive actions of our fellows on the outside. But this is not the case with all substances. There are some congregations of atoms through which the æther waves can make their way. Man calls such materials *transparent*; for example, glass and water are transparent substances. The fact of the matter is that in such substances none of us are able to respond to the incoming waves, and so we cannot stop them. I should say almost none of us, for there are always a few electrons present who happen to be in sympathy with the incoming waves. That is why no substance is perfectly transparent.

The point concerning which I wish to speak in particular is this. Although we allow the æther waves to pass through such substances, we do offer some slight resistance to the passage of the waves; the faster the to-and-fro motion of the waves, the more resistance do we offer. That is why the waves of highest frequency are bent farthest from the straight line when passed through a glass prism. We actually force the æther waves to travel slower through a piece of glass than through the air.

Now there should be no mystery concerning our action in a triangular piece of glass. Whatever combination of æther waves falls upon it, the different trains of waves are sorted out according to their frequencies. Suppose, for instance, that æther waves emitted from some incandescent sodium are passed through a glass prism. The bulk of the electrons attached to the sodium atoms are capable of revolving at speeds which produce waves causing the sensation of yellow. Hence there will appear a very distinct line of yellow light in the spectrum. But why should the light be in the form of a line? Simply because our æther waves are passed through a narrow slit in a shutter. But I need not trouble you with further details of our actions, which, although very simple to us, may seem somewhat strange to you.

You will understand, however, that we form bright lines in different parts of the spectrum, according to the kinds of atoms to which we are attached. It was this fact which attracted man's attention to our wireless messages. He soon discovered the meaning of these lines, for he commenced to take exact notes of the different positions in which we placed these lines. He saw that when we were attached to hydrogen atoms we always produced three prominent lines; a very distinct line in the red section, another in the blue part, and a third one somewhat fainter and farther along in the blue. On the other hand, when attached to sodium atoms, we produced two very distinct lines in the yellow. When attached to iron atoms we produced a great variety of lines in the spectrum. Of course these substances have to be incandescent to enable us to produce the æther waves.

Now it will be clear to you how we send wireless messages from the distant stars. These stars are great masses of flaming gases, so that the satellite electrons are kept busy dancing attendance to excited atoms. The electrons are constantly sending out æther waves, which reach this planet. We sort out these waves when man passes them through a glass prism, mounted in a telescope arrangement which he calls a *spectroscope*. He then examines the positions of the lines we produce in the resulting spectrum, and from these he knows what kinds of atoms are present in the distant star. It is we who have informed man that there are forty different materials in the sun, the most common of which are hydrogen, sodium, iron, copper, nickel, and zinc. Of course these all exist in a gaseous form.

There is one point about which I need hardly trouble you, although it is worth mentioning in passing. While we produce bright lines in the spectrum of any incandescent substance on this planet, our messages from the stars appear as dark lines. The reason for this is that there are cooler masses of the gases surrounding the incandescent masses forming the stars, and these cooler gases completely absorb the waves we produce. So completely are these waves absorbed that blank spaces are left in the spectrum, and these are the dark lines to which I refer. As they are in the same positions that the bright lines would have occupied had the waves reached the earth, it makes no difference to the reading of our messages.

Curiously enough, some of our actions in forming lines in the spectrum led to our actual discovery by man; but I shall tell you of this in the following chapter.

CHAPTER XVI

HOW MAN PROVED OUR EXISTENCE

How man reasoned out a plan for detecting the electron. How the electrons altered some lines in the spectrum. The curious manner in which the Electron informed man that certain stars are approaching this planet, while others are receding from it

THE SCRIBE'S NOTE ON CHAPTER SIXTEEN

Several men of note declared that "little particles" revolved around the atoms of matter, and that it was the motion of these particles which produced the well-known æther waves of light.

This idea was suggested by the result of certain mathematical calculations.

It was some time before real experimental proof was obtained.

The electron tells its own tale of this great discovery.

When the electron speaks of a spectrum line being shifted up or down the scale, it means towards the violet or the red end respectively.

We may picture the spectrum as analogous to the keyboard of a piano.

In the second part of this chapter, the electron explains how it has enabled man to discover that certain stars are approaching the earth, while others are receding from it.

We electrons had waited long ages for man to acknowledge our services, but we did not despise the acknowledgment which a few men accorded us upon the basis of their mathematical calculations. It was natural, however, that we should want something more definite than this.

You can imagine our joy when real experimental proof of our existence was established. Perhaps you think that we should have been satisfied with this. But even this did not bring acknowledgment from many outside scientific circles, and not even from all within those circles. As our services to man are universal, we feel that all men should become acquainted with our doings. Indeed that was the chief argument used by my fellow-electrons, who urged me to write this autobiography. The story of our actual discovery by man is an interesting one.

It all came about in a very simple manner, but in quite a different way from what most electrons expected. Man reasoned within himself that if we electrons really did revolve around atoms and thus produce waves in the æther, as had been suggested, he ought to be able to affect our movements by disturbing the æther in which we were revolving. Of course man cannot disturb the æther directly; he must employ some of us to do this for him. He caused us to produce a very powerful magnetic field, which, as you know, is a disturbance of the æther. Man did not bother thinking about *us* in this connection; he simply sent an electric current around an electro-magnet, but I have explained to you the very active part we play in electric and magnetic actions.

From my story in the preceding chapter, you are aware that man had observed the meaning of the bright lines in the spectrum of any incandescent body. When he examined the æther waves we send out from sodium atoms, he found two very distinct lines in the yellow. Because of the brightness of these lines, man selected a sodium flame to experiment with in the present case.

You will picture a great host of my fellow-electrons revolving around the atoms in a sodium flame. The flame was placed between the poles of a very powerful electro-magnet, and a beam of æther waves (light) produced by us was directed into the spectroscope. The experimenter focussed all his attention upon one of the bright yellow lines. He noted very carefully the exact position in which we placed it. He then produced the magnetic field around the flame, in which my fellow-electrons were revolving at a steady pace, and, behold, the line which he was watching split up into two lines, one taking up a position a little higher up the spectrum scale, and the other going a little lower down towards the red end. What could this mean?

Man had no difficulty in knowing the cause of this alteration; indeed, it was exactly what he had hoped would take place. Of the two new lines, one represented waves a little shorter, while the other line indicated waves a little longer or farther apart, than the original waves forming the single line. This could only come about by some of the electrons having had their rate of revolution increased, while that of others had been reduced. These alterations were due to the æther disturbance (the magnetic field). Those electrons whose orbits happened to lie in one position had their rate of revolution increased, while those whose orbits lay in another position had their speed reduced. Man was convinced at last that we "particles" were real existing things.

Whenever man withdrew the æther disturbance, the electrons fell back into their natural rate of revolution, and the original single line appeared in the spectrum.

I took no part in the original experiment which gave absolute proof of our existence, but since then I have been present in a laboratory when the same experiment has been repeated.

This is not the only case in which we alter the positions of definite lines in the spectrum. Indeed, we have given man some interesting information about the motions of distant stars—information which he could not have obtained in any other way. We have sent wireless messages from distant stars, indicating that they were approaching the earth, while electrons aboard other stars have signalled that they are receding from the earth. All this may seem mysterious to you, and yet our actions in the matter are very simple. Indeed, we do nothing but what I have told you of in the preceding chapters. We send out definite wave-lengths in the manner described already. But if we are on board a star which is travelling towards the earth, our waves will naturally follow a little closer at each other's heels. On the other hand, if the star is receding from the earth, the waves must be a little farther apart than they would be if the star were at rest.

You will understand that the electrons are revolving at the same speeds in both cases, but the forward movement of the star crowds the waves together, while a receding star stretches them out a little farther apart. The result at the receiving end is that the crowded waves are just as though they had come from electrons revolving at a greater speed than is actually the case. Hence the line appears farther along the spectrum, up the scale of frequencies, than would have been the case had the star not been moving forward in the line of sight. Thus if the hydrogen lines, of which I have spoken elsewhere, should appear higher up the spectrum than usual, then man knows that the star from which these waves are coming is approaching the earth.

It will be evident that when known lines in the spectrum are shifted down the scale (towards the red end of the spectrum), then the rate of the waves has been decreased, and man knows that the star carrying these stimulating electrons is receding from him.

You will observe that we electrons perform no new duty in connection with this matter; it is entirely the motion of the body carrying us that alters the positions of the lines. But I must hasten on to tell you of some personal experiences.

CHAPTER XVII
MY X-RAY EXPERIENCES

X-rays are an old story to some electrons. The Electron's personal experience. A very sudden stop. How electrons made a fluorescent screen send out light. The electrons assist the surgeon. A curious find. Detecting imitation diamonds. The Electron and the mummy

THE SCRIBE'S NOTE ON CHAPTER SEVENTEEN

The present generation were all very much interested in the discovery of X-rays.

With the aid of a battery and an induction coil, man causes an energetic electrical discharge to pass through a vacuum tube.

When the flying electrons strike upon a little metal target placed in their path, they produce the well-known Roentgen rays.

We have all become familiar with the great penetrating powers of these rays.

The electron may be left to tell its own story.

It was no surprise to us that we could produce what man calls X-rays, but we were very much surprised at the use to which man put these splashes which we made in the æther. A limited number of us had been producing X-rays on our own account for many ages, but I shall tell you of that in a later chapter, when you will hear how we made the world talk.

I must tell you of my own experiences in connection with these X-rays, which I hear some men describe also as *Roentgen rays*. I found myself once more within a large vacuum tube, and as soon as I felt a crowd of my fellows pushing me forward, I was quite prepared to be shot across the tube, as on previous occasions. Personally, I was not prepared for what was to come. Just as we reached the centre of the tube we collided with a metal plate or target. It was no joke to be pulled up so suddenly when travelling at a terrific speed. I noticed at the time that our very sudden stoppage had a peculiar effect upon the æther. Of course we never bothered about a name for this disturbance; it is man who requires to have names for everything. He was quite right to call this æther disturbance "X-rays," for even now he does not know the real nature of these. I have heard him describe them as thin pulses in the æther, but there is something more.

I may as well confess that although we observed this æther disturbance arising from our sudden stoppage, we paid little attention to it, until it became apparent that man was continuing to produce these rays for some special purpose. He had discovered that we could shoot these rays right through many solid substances which were not transparent to light. But I have not told you how man came to know that we could produce these penetrating rays.

On one occasion we were sending out these rays, which, by the way, do not cause any sensation in man's visionary apparatus. The room was in darkness. Some of the invisible rays fell upon a collection of small chemical crystals which were fixed on the surface of a screen. Our fellow-electrons, who were attached to the atoms of the crystals, were bestirred into action. They could not reflect the X-rays, but they set up regular trains of waves in the æther, some of which came within the range that affects man's vision. Man knew that this chemical screen could not produce light on its own account, and it became apparent that the vacuum tube must be sending some æther waves towards the chemical screen.

As the electrons on the screen produced an æther disturbance different from that which fell upon it, man called this a *fluorescent screen*.

At first we took merely a passing interest in the experiments which man made with these X-rays of ours, for it seemed to us as though man thought them only good enough for amusing his friends. Indeed, we paid little heed to what he was doing, until we observed that the rays were being used by surgeons. We were interested at once, for here we could serve man.

My first experience in this connection was quite interesting. A young girl had got a needle into her hand while she was playing about, and the surgeons were at a loss to know where the needle had lodged. We lost no time in producing X-rays which could penetrate the flesh of the hand, and reach the fluorescent screen on the other side. The bones of the hand blocked the way of our rays, but not so completely as the needle did. Hence we produced upon the screen a faint shadow of the flesh of the hand, a much deeper image of the bones, and a black shadow of the needle. This enabled the surgeon to see where the needle was hiding.

Sometimes we were called upon to produce rays for detecting bullets in the flesh, or for showing the nature of a fractured bone. We were never surprised to find that our call was to detect a coin in the throat of a child, but in this connection a big surprise awaited some of us. I was not one of the party, but I have the information from some fellow-electrons.

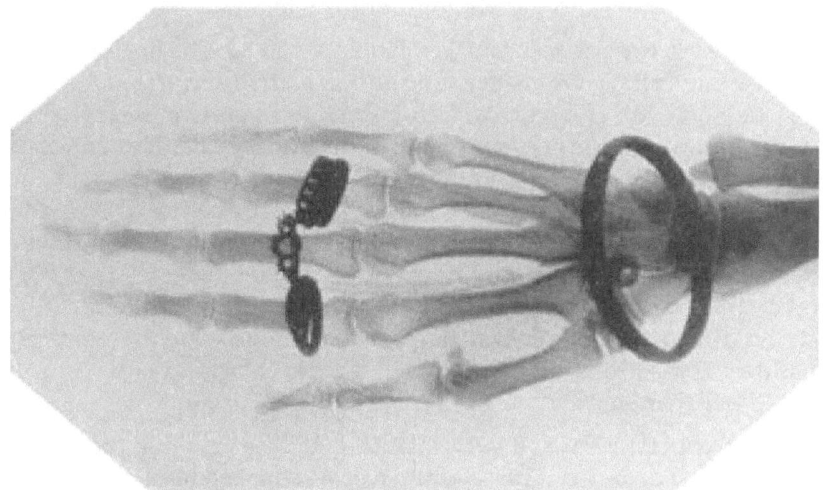

How Electrons Produce X-Ray Images

The upper photograph shows the X-ray apparatus in use. The operator is examining the bones of the lady's hand, which she places between the X-ray tube and the fluorescent screen. The rays pass through the flesh, but are obstructed by the bones, the rings, and the bangle, so that a shadowgraph or image is formed upon the screen, which becomes luminous where the rays succeed in reaching it. The actual examination is made in a dark room. Owing to the way X-ray photos are taken (by contact) the image is reversed in a photograph, so that a left looks like a right hand.

A party of electrons were present within an X-ray tube at a large hospital, when they were called upon to produce rays for examining the throat of a little girl. They had become so used to this call that they did not doubt there would be a coin in the child's throat. However, they lost no time in producing the penetrating rays, and you can imagine their surprise when they produced the image of a toy bicycle upon the screen. It seemed ridiculous that such a toy could have entered a child's throat.

When we had shown the surgeons exactly where the toy was, they set to work to remove it. The electrons heard later that the operation was successful in every way. Every one was interested, and we were proud. I do not wish to appear boastful, but I wonder how many operations owe their success to these rays which we produce for man.

It was natural that man should try if these searching rays could affect the chemicals upon a photographic plate, and we soon proved that they could. It made no difference to us whether man kept the plate sealed up in its light-proof envelope, or whether he placed the plate within a wooden box. These protecting covers offered no barrier to our rays. We produced shadowgraphs of any objects placed between our tube and the photographic plate.

Two of my early experiences may be of interest to you. The first of these seemed to me a rather tame affair. Our X-ray tube appeared to be arranged for the amusement of fashionable folk. One grand lady placed her hand behind the fluorescent screen, whereupon we produced an image of the bones of her hand and very dark images of all the many rings upon her fingers. Several of the rings had enormous diamonds, but it was after she had gone away that I overheard two gentlemen speaking about the rings. One asked the other if he had observed the beautiful diamonds, whereupon the other roared with laughter. It seems that we proved them to be imitation diamonds, for our rays could not penetrate them, whereas they have no difficulty in passing through real diamonds. We therefore produced black shadows of the imitation diamonds. Little did the grand lady know how we had exposed her sham jewels.

My second experience was a very curious one. I learned that our tube was being carried to some distance. After a while we were placed beside a peculiar-looking object, which the men referred to as the "mummy." One of the men suggested that they should photograph its feet, but before doing so they darkened the room and set us to work upon the fluorescent screen. The owner of the mummy got rather nervous as to what we might disclose, and as the force urging us into action was somewhat erratic at first, we produced only a very indistinct image. We were greatly amused at the nervous excitement of the owner; he seemed to think our verdict was that there were no bones. However, the man with the apparatus soon got things into better condition, and this enabled us to produce X-rays satisfactorily. The result was that they secured some excellent photographs of the hidden bones of the mummy.

Before telling you how we made the world talk, I should like to give you a clear idea of our relationship to the atoms of matter.

CHAPTER XVIII
OUR RELATIONSHIP TO THE ATOMS

How the atoms of matter attract one another. What constitutes the temperature of a body. What the atoms are made of. An important thing still to discover about the atom. The elements. How the electrons produce compound substances. The real explanation of chemical changes

THE SCRIBE'S NOTE ON CHAPTER EIGHTEEN

We have no doubt that an atom of matter is a miniature solar system of revolving electrons.

These electrons, being negative particles of electricity, would repel each other just as any two similarly electrified bodies do.

There must therefore be some equivalent of positive electricity, but whether this exists in the form of a sphere or in separate particles we have no definite knowledge.

One atom differs from another in the number of electrons which go to make up the atom.

The electron explains how the atoms of matter are united to one another, how different compound substances are formed, and how chemical changes take place.

I am sorry that this part of my story must remain incomplete for the present. I am not free to tell you all I know; you must try and get behind the scenes on your own account.

One thing I am at liberty to tell you is that my fellow-electrons who are locked up within the atoms are not without hope that they may gain their freedom once more at some future time. I know this first-hand, for I have met some fellow-electrons who have escaped from within an atom, but I shall delay telling you about these fellows till the succeeding chapter. My object in mentioning this fact now is to give you confidence in what I am about to say regarding the nature of the atom.

On one occasion I overheard a conversation between two men who were discussing the construction of matter. One remarked that the atoms were the bricks of the universe, whereupon the other asked how the little bricks were cemented together. I wish that man could have seen a lump of matter as we see it. He would have been surprised to learn that the atoms never really touch each other. They are always surging to and fro, or *vibrating*, and it is this motion which constitutes the *temperature* of the body which they compose.

It must be clear, however, that in a solid body one atom attracts another atom across the intervening atomic spaces. This is another duty devolving upon us; what we do, really, is to upset the electric balance between the different atoms, and thus produce electrical attraction.

First of all, perhaps, I should explain that the different kinds of atoms are simply congregations of different numbers of electrons. Of course there is the other part, of which I am forbidden to speak—the part which man vaguely describes as *positive electricity*. However, you may take it from me that while it is true that the main difference between an atom of gold and an atom of iron, or of oxygen, is in the number of electrons it contains, there is a very important difference in the arrangement of the electrons. You know that they form rings outside one another, all of which revolve at enormous speeds. The number of electrons in the different rings varies according to the kind of atom.

It is quite correct for man to speak of the atoms containing certain definite numbers of electrons, but I should like you to understand clearly that the exact number of electrons is not permanently fixed; one or more electrons can slip off one atom and become attached to a neighbouring atom which happens to be capable of accepting it or them. It is the interchange of these few detachable electrons that causes one atom to attract another. In other words, it is the differently charged atoms which attract each other, just as man crowds a surplus of electrons on to one object and finds it attracted bodily towards another object having a deficiency of electrons.

It is this electrical attraction between the atoms which enables us to build up the particles, or *molecules*, of matter in such a variety of forms. First of all, we play the most important part within the atoms. We have formed only a limited number of such atoms. I am not free to tell you exactly how many, for man has discovered only about eighty of these different congregations of electrons, each kind of which he calls an *element*. The way in which we have coupled these different elementary atoms together must appear remarkable to all thinking men; there seems to be no end to the possible variety of combinations.

In one case we unite an atom of *chlorine* to an atom of *sodium* and thereby produce a molecule of common salt. In another case we unite an atom of *oxygen* to two atoms of *hydrogen*, and the resulting combination is an invisible molecule of ordinary water.

It has always seemed to me very strange how some men have difficulty in regard to these combinations. I have heard a man ask how two different gases, hydrogen and oxygen, when united, should form a liquid, and not a gas. I wish you could see things as we see them. The atoms are neither gaseous, liquid, nor solid; they are little worlds of revolving electrons.

I have spoken of the attraction between atoms, and again between molecules, in form ing a solid body. It will be clear that there is less of this *cohesive force* in the case of a liquid, whereas it is absent entirely in the case of a gas. In this case the molecules have become so far separated from one another that they cease to attract each other, and if left free they will soon part company, and spread themselves broadcast over the face of the earth.

Whether a substance passes into a solid, a liquid, or a gaseous state, the atoms remain constant, but their vibratory motion is altered very considerably. However, I was about to tell you that we electrons can make some very interesting combinations of atoms. Those I have mentioned so far are of a very simple nature, but we have built up individual molecules containing hundreds of atoms. We link about a hundred atoms together and produce a molecule of what man calls *alum*, and we require to unite about a thousand atoms together to make one molecule of *albumen* (the white of an egg).

When man speaks of a chemical change having taken place in a substance, it is simply the electrons who have made a friendly interchange of detachable electrons, thereby causing a different assemblage of the same atoms. During these changes we never alter the nature of the atom. That little world of revolving electrons known as an atom of gold, remains always an atom of gold. But you must not run away with the idea that the atoms will never change. Indeed, man has discovered that the atoms are not eternal, as I shall explain in the following chapter.

CHAPTER XIX
HOW WE MADE THE WORLD TALK

It was nothing new on the part of the electrons. Exaggerated rumours. The electrons and radium. Fast-flying electrons. Atomic explosions

THE SCRIBE'S NOTE ON CHAPTER NINETEEN

The discovery of radium is within the memory of all.

Many exaggerated statements went abroad at the outset, but the real facts are full of interest, and they have shed much new light on many subjects.

Three different kinds of radiation were found to be emitted by radium.

At first man could not tell what these were, so he named them after the first three letters of the Greek alphabet—Alpha, Beta, and Gamma, rays.

The electron tells the interesting story of these rays, and relates the experiences of some fellow-electrons who escaped from within a radium atom.

We electrons were amused at the stir which we unconsciously caused throughout the civilised world. We had done nothing different from what we had been doing for ages, but a few men had been taking note of what we were about, and when the phenomena to which I refer became known to the world, many wild rumours were circulated.

One of these rumours was to the effect that steam-engines and their expensive furnaces were to disappear very quickly. If the two last words had been omitted—I should not say that the prophecy is untrue, but man has a long way to travel yet before reaching that goal. My fellows within the atoms have sufficient energy to supply all mankind with power if he could but unlock even a small fraction of it.

Another statement was that this newly discovered substance, *radium*, could cure some diseases which man had believed to be incurable. All I shall say about this is that the statement was an exaggerated one.

Then it was said that radium disproved much of man's scientific knowledge, but instead of that being so, we electrons have greatly extended man's knowledge by our radio-active actions. If any man believed the atoms of matter to be eternal, we certainly disproved that. Here, in radium, man could see atoms going to pieces.

I have questioned a fellow-electron who escaped from a radium atom as to what upset their equilibrium, but I find that he does not know, or he pretends not to know. All he has told me is that he was flung off suddenly from within the atom with great energy, for he had been revolving at a tremendous speed. In his sudden flight he passed some newly formed *helium* atoms, which contained many of those electrons who had been his co-partners in the former radium atom. Being an electron, he was travelling at a far greater speed than these flying atoms of matter, but he assures me that these helium atoms were going faster than atoms can travel under any other circumstances.

Another thing that this escaped electron told me was that when he and his fellow-electrons made a sudden start on leaving the atom of radium they caused a proper splash in the surrounding æther, just such as we electrons produce when we are suddenly stopped in an X-ray tube. Man observed these rays proceeding from radium, but, not knowing the cause of them, he called them *gamma rays*. We can, of course, produce radiographs when these rays fall upon photographic plates. Indeed, some of my fellow-electrons, when escaping from radium, have produced rays sufficient to penetrate a six-inch boulder and affect a photographic plate lying beneath the boulder. In time man recognised these rays as X-rays.

Man did not find only these rays—he discovered that electrons were escaping, but before he had recognised what we were, he had named us *beta rays*. These fast-flying electrons have had experiences which never fall to electrons except when escaping from an atom. Their velocity is so great that they can be shot right through a sheet of aluminium foil. If these escaped electrons are allowed to settle on any object, they will necessarily cause an overcrowding, or, in other words, the object will become negatively electrified.

The one thing that puzzled man most was to find out what the helium atoms were. He had named them *alpha* rays, but as he found he could not get them to penetrate even a thin sheet of paper, he was confident that they must be atoms of matter. It was only when he had gathered sufficient to examine the spectrum that he found these to be helium atoms.

I think what really made the world talk was the fact that electrons were escaping from what had been supposed to be an eternal habitation. In other words, this material radium was actually going to pieces. That is to say, *gradually*, as far as man is concerned, for, looking at it from our point of view, the word *gradual* seems out of place entirely. The breaking up of an atom is really of the nature of an explosion. It is a continual bombardment that is proceeding in radium. Why man is apt to think of it as a gradual effect is that there is such an enormous number of atoms in a tiny speck of radium, that even the incessant series of explosions will take a very long time to break down the whole of the small particle.

Electrons differ in their opinions as to whether man will succeed in drawing upon this internal energy of the atom. My own difficulty is that, having been a roaming electron at all times, I have no idea regarding the cause of the atomic explosions. I have remarked already that the electrons locked up within the atoms possess more energy than man could ever use. If all these electrons were deprived of their energy, the atoms of matter would cease to exist, and man, where would he be?

CHAPTER XX
CONCLUSION

The Electron is made to sum up a few of the wonders which it has
related, in order to emphasise the great services which electrons
render to man

THE SCRIBE'S NOTE ON CHAPTER TWENTY

Not many of us have realised the true importance of electrons in the Creator's plans.

In the following short chapter the electron is made to sum up a few of the wonders which it has related, in order to focus our attention upon the grand place which the electrons occupy in the universe.

From what I have told you of myself and my fellow-electrons, it must be apparent that we are of tremendous importance to man. I have told you something of the part we played in building up this world—how we not only form the atoms of matter, but also hold these bricks of the universe together. I have given you a rough sketch of the composition of these bricks.

You must have realised also that without us the whole universe would be in darkness. There would be no light, no heat, and consequently no life. Indeed, there could be no material existence without us.

Where would man be if we failed to perform our mission? He could not exist if we even neglected a few of our duties. Not only do we form the atoms of which his body is composed, also holding these together, but we produce all those chemical changes within his body which are absolutely necessary to maintain life. His very thoughts are dependent upon our activities.

I have told you how we send man's messages across the earth, and how we transmit power from place to place. Also how we have enabled man to gain knowledge of the distant stars, and to examine the bones of his living body.

If man could cross-examine me or any of my fellows, I expect the first question would be—What are you electrons made of? But man must find this out for himself. The Creator has placed man in a world full of activity, and it is of intense interest to man to discover the meaning of all that lies around him. That is why I have been bound over by my fellows to tell you only so much of our history as man has discovered. But I am disclosing no secret when I admit that our very existence as electrons is dependent upon the æther.

If I can find another scribe to write a revised biography for me a few hundred years hence, I shall have a much more interesting tale to tell, for many of our doings, of which man knows nothing at present, will be secrets no longer by that time.

APPENDIX

THE SCRIBE'S NOTE ON APPENDIX

As explained by the author in Chapter I., this appendix has been added for the sake of those readers who may wish further details than have been given in the electron's story.

It is only necessary to give a brief notice of the more important particulars, as the author has written recently upon this subject in a popular form.[1]

It was known two thousand years ago that when a piece of amber was rubbed with a woollen cloth, the amber would attract light objects towards it. Amber was considered to be unique in this respect.

About the year 1600, one of Queen Elizabeth's physicians, Dr. William Gilbert, inquired into this attractive property of amber. He found that many other substances possessed the same property. Indeed it is common to all substances in some degree. We say the amber or other object is "electrified."

It was observed by the early experimenters that there were two kinds of electrification. To one of these they gave the name *positive electricity*, and to the other *negative electricity*.

Every electrified object will attract an object which is not electrified, and two objects which are oppositely electrified will attract one another also. But two objects which are similarly electrified will repel each other.

Man got tired of rubbing objects by hand, so he fitted up simple machines in which glass cylinders or plates were rubbed against leather cushions. The electricity was then collected by little metal points supported on an insulated metal sphere.

The experiment of attempting to store electricity in a glass vessel filled with water was made at the University of Leyden (Netherlands). The water was replaced later by a coating of tin-foil on the inner surface, while a similar metallic coating on the outside took the place of the experimenter's hand. These jars are called *Leyden jars*, after the place in which the discovery was made.

About 1790, Professor Galvani, of Italy, observed that the legs of a freshly killed frog twitched at each discharge of an electrical machine. Later he found that the same twitching occurred when he connected certain parts with a piece of copper and zinc. He believed this to be due to "animal electricity" secreted within

---

[1] "Scientific Ideas of To-day." By Chas. R. Gibson, F.R.S.E. (London: Seeley & Co., Ltd. Five shillings net.)

the frog.

Professor Volta, also of Italy, proved that Galvani's idea was wrong, and that the electricity resided in the metals rather than in the frog. He showed that when two pieces of dissimilar metal were put in contact with one another, there was a slight transference of electricity between them. He constructed a pile of copper and zinc discs, with a moist cloth between each pair or couple, and by connecting wires from the top copper disc to the lowest zinc disc he was able to show that an appreciable current of electricity was produced. Later he placed a piece of copper and a piece of zinc in a vessel containing acidulated water, whereupon he found that a steady current of electricity was obtained. This was the invention of electric batteries.

The phenomena of *magnetism* were known to the ancients, but it was not until the nineteenth century that we found any real connection between electricity and magnetism. In 1819, a Danish philosopher, Hans Christian Oersted, discovered that an electric current passing in a wire affected a magnet in its neighbourhood. If the magnet was supported on a pivot, after the manner of a compass needle, it would turn round and take up a position at right angles to the wire carrying the electric current.

The molecular theory of magnetism presumes that every molecule of iron is a tiny magnet, having a north and south pole. In a piece of unmagnetised iron, these tiny magnets are all lying so that they neutralise one another. When they are turned round so that their north poles are all lying in one direction, then the iron is said to be magnetised.

The electron theory of magnetism does not do away with the older molecular theory just referred to. The electron theory goes a step farther, and tells us that these molecules are magnets because of a steady motion of electrons around the atoms of iron.

It was discovered in 1825 that when an electric current was sent through an insulated wire wound around a piece of soft iron, the iron became a magnet; when the current was stopped the magnetism disappeared. Such magnets are called *electro-magnets*. If a piece of hard steel is treated in the same way it becomes a *permanent magnet*. It was this intimate connection between electricity and magnetism, or, in other words, the invention of these electro-magnets, which brought us electric bells, telegraphs, telephones, dynamos, and electric motors.

It should be noted that while iron is attracted by either pole of a magnet, there is such a thing as magnetic repulsion. This, however, takes place only between two magnets, and then only between like poles.

Some German physicists made a number of electrical experiments with vacuum tubes. When Sir William Crookes (England) was experimenting with similar vacuum tubes he suggested that matter was in a "radiant" state during the electric discharge within the tubes.

In 1880, H. A. Lorentz, of Amsterdam, declared that light was due to the motion of small particles revolving around the atoms of matter.

Professor Zeeman, of Holland, produced experimental proof of Lorentz's theory. He showed that the revolving "particles" were influenced by a powerful magnetic field, in the manner explained in the electron's story. This discovery was made in 1896, or sixteen years after Lorentz's declaration. It was Dr. Johnstone Stoney, of Dublin University (Ireland), who christened these particles "electrons."

The X-rays were observed for the first time by Professor Roentgen, of Germany, in 1895. The screens used for viewing the luminous effects produced by the X-rays are coated with very fine crystals of *barium platinocyanide*. These screens were in use for another purpose previous to the discovery of X-rays.

We know now that *chemical affinity* is merely electrical attraction between the atoms of matter.

The spectroscope consists of a glass prism, or series of prisms, mounted between two metal tubes. One tube is provided at one end with a vertical slit, through which the light that is to be examined is passed. At the other end of the tube is a lens, so that the beam of light from the slit emerges through the lens as a pencil of parallel rays. The pencil of light then falls upon the glass prism, striking it at an angle. In passing through the prism, the light is bent round so that it enters the second tube, which is simply a small telescope. The prism separates the æther waves according to their wave-lengths, and produces the well-known coloured spectrum, which is magnified by the telescope. The reason for the bending of the different waves is explained in the electron's story.

Lector House believes that a society develops through a two-fold approach of continuous learning and adaptation, which is derived from the study of classic literary works spread across the historic timeline of literature records. Therefore, we aim at reviving, repairing and redeveloping all those inaccessible or damaged but historically as well as culturally important literature across subjects so that the future generations may have an opportunity to study and learn from past works to embark upon a journey of creating a better future.

This book is a result of an effort made by Lector House towards making a contribution to the preservation and repair of original ancient works which might hold historical significance to the approach of continuous learning across subjects.

HAPPY READING & LEARNING!

LECTOR HOUSE LLP
E-MAIL: lectorpublishing@gmail.com